Game Gun

GAME GUN

RICHARD S. GROZIK

© 1986, 1997, 2002 by Richard S. Grozik

All rights reserved. No part of this publication may be reproduced or transmitted in any form or by any means, electronic or mechanical, including photocopy, recording, or any information storage or retrieval systems, without permission in writing from the author, except by a reviewer, who may quote brief passages in a critical article or review to be printed in a magazine or newspaper or electronically transmitted on radio or television.

Published by

Krause Publications
700 East State Street, Iola, WI 54990-0001
Telephone (715) 445-2214
www.krause.com

Please call or write for our free catalog of publications.
Our toll-free number to place an order or obtain a free catalog is (800) 258-0929.

Library of Congress Catalog Card Number: 2002105093
ISBN: 0-87349-513-6

Printed in the United States of America

To those who know the indescribable joy of the hunt

CONTENTS

Acknowledgments		ix
Foreword		xi
Introduction		xiii
1	The Upland Gun	1
2	A Fit Gun	13
3	Metal to Metal	33
4	Good Wood	71
5	Steel Tapestry	93
6	American Made	115
7	The Modern Classics	133
8	Over-Under	157
9	The Gun Room	169
	Glossary	185
	Gun Dealers, Makers, and Master Craftsmen	193

ACKNOWLEDGMENTS

Although this book is a very personal statement, many persons were responsible for its completion. I am deeply indebted to the late John Amber for his editing insights; to Art DeLaurier Jr. for his production talents; to master craftsmen Ron Collings, David Catchpole, Nick Makinson, Kirk Merrington, Tony Tomlinson, David Trevallion, Hunt Turner, and Fred Wenig for their willingness to share the tricks of the trade; to hunter-artist Joseph Fornelli for his encouragement and counsel; to hunting companions Denny Palm, Glenn Chambers, and Frank Ehrenford whose friendship I cherish; and to my wife and family, who endured the labor pains that gave birth to *Game Gun*. Special thanks is also given to Dave Morrison, Bill Moore (William Larkin Moore), Winston Churchill, John A. Grozik, Peter Miller, John Corry, Joseph Fornelli, William W. Headrick, and Ducks Unlimited for the photography that appears throughout this book.

Foreword

What is a true game gun? To me it is a key element in the enjoyment of the art that is wingshooting. When properly brought together to complete the triad of bird, dog, and gun, it can help elevate wingshooting from the mere hunting of game to a nearly religious experience.

The game gun is more than a tool for gathering game birds or hitting clay targets. It is a reflection of the owner's personality and attitude about his sport. As such, it can be highly ornate or quietly elegant. In either case the true game gun is the perfect marriage of art and function. It is this combination of beauty and deadly efficiency which separates best-quality guns from the mass-produced firearms that are so prevalent today. The sporting pursuit of a noble game bird with a courageous, well-trained gun dog and a finely crafted shotgun is the completion of a work of art each time it takes place.

You can easily understand why when *Game Gun* was first introduced in 1986 I eagerly snapped up the first copy I could get my hands on. The thought of an entire book dedicated to fine guns was exciting to me, because the introduction of *Game Gun* coincided with my early symptoms of double-gun fever, which eventually lead me from a solid, secure engineering job to the fascinating but volatile world of gun trading. I can honestly say that I was not disappointed in the book. It was informative and educational, and it taught me more about the process of producing a fine double gun than I had learned in my previous ten years of haphazard gun collecting and trading combined. It was evident that *Game Gun* was written by someone who not only understood the technical function of guns, but who also had a love and appreciation for the skill and artistry of the craftsmen who built and decorated these guns we all coveted.

In this newer, revised edition of *Game Gun,* Rich Grozik has expanded the book to include the over-under and its growing importance to the shooting community. He has also expanded and improved the chapter on gunfitting. This chapter alone is a great reason to purchase the book. Rich gives good, common-sense advice on gunfitting without making it seem like black magic or the high science that some instructors would have you believe it to be. He has expanded and modernized several other chapters to reflect recent changes in the gun trade. The heart of this book, however, remains the same. It is a wonderful educational resource for anyone wanting to learn the facts behind the myths of fine sporting guns.

Rich is an experienced shooter with a great love and understanding of his topic. He has instructed and entertained so many of us with his articles and with the original edition of *Game Gun*. I am sure this second edition will add to the success of the first. One thing is certain, this new edition is sure to start an epidemic of double-gun fever in a new generation of shooters.

—John Allen
Game Fair
Nashville, Tennessee

Introduction

I WAS DAYDREAMING ABOUT DUCKS more than I was hunting pheasants as I watched my setter chase his nose down last year's corn rows. The black soil was soft underfoot, some of it taking my boots for a ride and slowing me to a shuffle. A bright autumn sun glared at me enough to keep my eyes to the ground and my thoughts on the approaching nor'easter that would surely bring ducks. The waterfowl season opened soon, and there were blinds to brush, decoys to rig, and calls to practice. A flushing ringneck could have had some fun with my reflexes in that October cornfield, while I mused about a successful opener in the marsh.

By accident or by fate, as I neared a fence rail at the end of the field, my eyes caught a flash of white cradled in a dirt clod; something that had eluded me for years, I found in an instant. There, as if just dropped, was a delicately sculptured arrowhead. I picked it up, rubbed it clean, admired its almost perfect form, and let out a whoop that surprised both me and my dog. It was as if something sacred had reached out across the ages to remind me of a hunting heritage that was man's long before gunpowder. I thought a little about how the pointed artifact might have come to rest, unharmed, in the field—a place hunted by a man more primitive, yet in many other ways more privileged, than myself—and continued my halfhearted pursuit of pheasants. I never did feel much weight in my game bag that day, but I left that windblown hunting ground with a handful of history and a deeper respect for my origins.

Man the hunter has prevailed because he is nature's archetype. He is the original experiment in perfected form and function. His tools of the hunt have become extensions of his physical and social survival. The modern hunter has changed little since prehistoric times. Though technology has enhanced his pursuit of game, it has not changed either his biological or spiritual need to hunt.

Today's game guns are the ultimate expression of the predatory instinct man has refined over thousands of years. His reverence for the game he hunted then was reflected in cave paintings and intricately crafted spear points as it is captured now in engraved game scenes found on the sidelocks of skillfully wrought sporting arms.

One of man's highest art forms, game guns combine the utility of function with the artistry of carved wood and engraved steel. They complement the eons of trial and error in game-tool development borne out of man's innate desire to hunt.

The personal statements found throughout this book are an attempt to recognize the labor of nameless men who struggled to elevate implements of the hunt to perfection. It will also offer basic instruction to today's hunter on what to expect from a properly built upland game gun. This book is not intended as a blueprint for budding gunsmiths, but rather as a study in game gun appreciation. Its primary focus concerns the creation of a classic side-by-side, sidelock shotgun. However, many characteristics of a game gun's construction can be applied to carefully crafted firearms of any configuration. Such

fine tools of the hunt have always demanded the best of man's creative ability. To those who seek adventure in the hunt and beauty in the sporting arms they carry, the past is indeed prologue to man's hunting future.

—Richard S. Grozik

A. H. Fox AE Grade special order 20-gauge. Photo by William W. Headrick, courtesy of Lewis Drake & Associates.

1

The Upland Gun

With uncompromising quality haunting their craft, today's game gun builders, whether in England, Spain, France, Germany, Italy, or the United States, offer hunters firearms as efficient in form and function as the game they hunt. There exists a universal unwritten law that unites all game gun makers: the quest for perfection. It is the single ingredient that separates all imitators from the original.

As early as the late 1700s, the concept of mating wood to metal in what has been termed the "classic" style has been explored by numerous gunmakers including the famed English gunmaker, Joseph Manton. Manton's side-by-side muzzleloaders reflected an economy of form and a functional elegance that remain a standard of comparison for all the great names in gunmaking today. Just as America pioneered and perfected the rifle and revolver, England has refined the double shotgun (sidelock and boxlock) to the degree that it has been emulated by gunmakers worldwide. So pure is its design, that almost the only improvements to be made exist in the realm of advanced metallurgy and minor cosmetic embellishment.

Inherent in the anatomy of an English "best" game gun are three very fundamental, interrelated elements on which successful wingshooting hinges: ease in mounting, pointability, and balance. Because hunted game is in motion, properly built game guns must possess dynamic handling qualities that allow the hunter to intercept flying birds with a minimum of effort. Contrary to popular belief, machines cannot quite duplicate the subtle refinements that generations of skilled hands can impart to wood and steel, animating it beyond sterile machine tolerances.

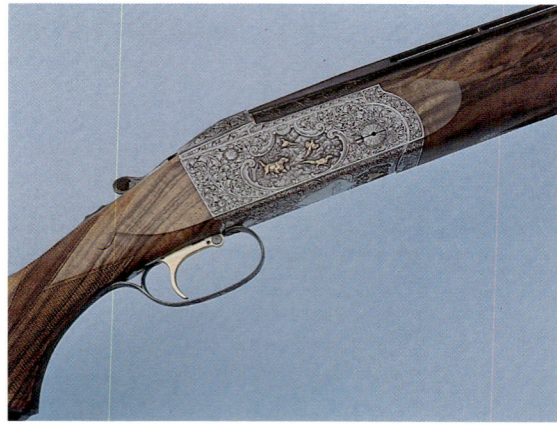

There exist in Europe today noted gunmakers whose sophisticated machinery has, except for final assembly, all but eliminated the discerning eye of the artisan. And while outwardly these ornately finished products may be capable of stirring the soul, they lack that intangible quality found in handmade guns. Their laboratory-like perfection often denies them the balance, fluid grace, and lively feel accorded game guns built by skilled hands; precision alone does not make a perfect gun.

English "best" game guns are still the standard-bearers for the trade. Such storied gunmakers as Purdey, Holland & Holland, Boss, and Churchill have, for more than a century, created game guns that attract discriminating shotgunners. Their collective knowledge of wood, metal characteristics, engraving art, and finishing techniques could fill a library as easily as their exquisitely crafted guns could fill a museum.

Sales talk aside, the English "best" has endured because it has followed a pure and simple tenet: adapt the firearm to the natural morphology of the shooter. Straight-grip stocks and slender forearms complement hand-eye coordination like no other design. Pistol grips and ponderous forearms serve only to depress the instinctive response of hand to gun, and eye to target. And while some may argue that the differences are too subtle to be measured, the experienced shooter can immediately feel the difference. Handling dynamics, then, is one of the game gun's greatest credentials. Such responsiveness cannot merely be added *on* to a gun, it must be built *into* it, piece by piece, until the whole becomes more than the sum of its many parts.

Because nearly all upland bird shooting is done with considerable body and reflex action, proper gun mounting is crucial to consistency afield. The custom fit of a classic, straight-grip game gun enables the shooter, with a little practice, to minimize wasted effort in bringing buttstock to shoulder. Rising birds should be met with rising barrels, and the uplifting, high-pointing virtues of a straight-stocked game gun lend themselves naturally to most upland bird shooting situations. Since the shoulder is really the triggering mechanism of an accomplished shooter—the gun being fired a split second after mounting—the gun must react almost involuntarily with the hunter's reflexes. Anyone who has hunted grouse, woodcock, or quail in thick cover can attest to the value of quick reflexes and a fast-mounting gun.

It is interesting to note the degree to which fashion has fueled the popularity of guns and shooting throughout history, especially in England. Were it not for royalty's love affair with "top hat" shooting during the late eighteenth and nineteenth centuries, game gun

makers of the period would have been hard pressed to peddle their costly products.

While much of the population was busy scrounging for an existence, England's thin upper crust provided the funds to perpetuate the manufacture and refinement of the modern game gun. "Top hat" shooting, as the name implies, referred to the fashionable high-crown hats of the era and was a forerunner of today's live pigeon and trapshooting. Wood pigeons were placed under top hats and released on command of the shooter, the top hat simply being "pulled" from over the bird by a string. England's gentry has a long tradition of involvement in the shooting sports, and to this day sets the gunning climate on the British Isles as well as in Europe.

With considerably less blue blood, America, too, has its royalty of sorts. From industrial giants and western movie greats to southern oil magnates and textile kings, the U.S. elite's social acceptability has often been tied to exclusive waterfowl club leases and elegant quail plantations. Their guns reflected the opulence of the era as well, with more than a few A-1 Parkers, Lefevers, L. C. Smith Deluxe grades, and Fox high grades making the rounds.

Before America's masses were educated and put on wheels, its well-heeled minority rode trains to week-long stays at the better hunting grounds around the nation. Ironically, the same mass-production philosophy that gilded the pockets of those early barons of industry and spawned the repeating shotgun would soon seal the fate of the American side-by-side and denude, with saw, plow, and drainpipe, the habitat that provided so much game for the gun. But the pendulum has swung once again in favor of the classic game gun. Shooters are demanding quality sporting arms and gunning experiences that are best served by hand-built double shotguns.

It has been said that American shotgun design was influenced a great deal by this nation's love affair with the rifle. America's affinity for pistol-grip shotgun stocks has especially been attributed to the country's strong rifle orientation. Yet when one researches America's early muzzleloading Kentuckys, single-shot Sharps, and lever-action Winchesters, not a pistol grip will be found among them. Even the early repeating shotguns, such as Browning's Auto-5 and Winchester's Model 12, were fitted with straight grips.

The pistol-grip shotgun stock in America emerged late in the nineteenth century and became well established in Charles Parker's line of "Old Reliables," Dan Lefever's sidelocks, and Remington side-by-sides. Perhaps the pistol grip was promoted more by America's early shotgun design than by the rifle-shooting fraternity. Whatever its origin, the full-pistol grip is better left to rifle stocks. Shotguns destined for upland bird shooting are better equipped with straight-grip or, at the very least, semi-pistol-grip stocks.

The British cling to straight-grip, splinter-forearmed shotguns for a very sound reason: they enable a shooter's hands to work in tandem throughout the gun-mounting procedure. Although a pistol-grip stock gives the rear hand a greater feeling of control over the gun, unless it is coupled with a beefy forearm to bring the leading hand onto the same plane, instinctive pointing is inhibited. According to the English, both hands, especially the leading, must work together to control, mount, and point the shotgun.

It is possible that America's turn-of-the-century "heads-up" style of shotgunning favored the pistol-grip stock as well as the exaggerated drop dimensions at the comb and heel. Also, the American shotgun was initially a multi-purpose gun used on everything from vermin and furred game to upland birds and waterfowl. The British, on the other hand, have always been a nation preoccupied with "shooting flying." The upland game gun is a specialty instrument designed specifically to kill flying birds. In Europe, notably Germany and Austria, shotgun design parallels the American preference for pistol-grip side-by-sides. The German predilection for shooting red stag and wild boar on private estates also gave rise to combination rifle-shotguns (drillings, etc.), cheekpiece stocks, and sling mounts on buttstocks and barrels.

In France, where "shooting flying" originated, game gun design closely adheres to the English tradition. Other sporting gun countries, such as Belgium, Spain, and Italy, also reflect England's classic game gun lines. It is interesting to note that hunters in these countries are also primarily upland bird shooters.

Whether boxlock or sidelock, game guns destined for the uplands should have their weight distributed between the hands.

Double shotguns built for driven-bird shooting often have straighter stocks and considerably less drop at the comb and heel than those built for "walk-up" bird shooting. Due to the speed of driven birds, and the angles at which they must be shot, many shooters prefer the built-in lead that straighter stock dimensions give them. As such, driven-bird guns can also be adapted for use on flushing pheasants or for jump shooting waterfowl.

However, these attributes can cause the same hunter to overshoot flat-flying targets such as quail, Hungarian partridge, or sharptailed grouse. Like it or not, there is really no such thing as an all-purpose shotgun. Shooting situations vary, and to take proper advantage of them all requires more than one shotgun. I, for one, will use every excuse available to add another game gun to the rack.

American gunmakers still build shotgun stocks with shorter length of pull and greater drop dimensions than do the British, but the trend is changing. Some of the special-edition Winchester Model 23 side-by-sides have been built with straighter, longer stocks for upland bird shooters.

In England's wide-open grouse moors and rambling shooting estates, long-stocked shotguns are shouldered with ease. But the same guns can be a bit difficult to mount in the close quarters of America's grouse and woodcock thickets. So, American game gun makers tend to shorten up their stocks as well as increase drop dimensions.

The English-designed game gun, then, has evolved out of a desire to wed the animate with the inanimate and has endured, simply, because it has succeeded. Although radical gunmaking concepts will continue to emerge from time to time, they will be continually overwhelmed by the simple, deadly symmetry of the classic game gun.

There is no denying that arguments can be made for other types of sporting shotguns; all have their allies. However, when superior balance, portability, choke selection, and overall handling dynamics are taken into consideration, a quality built side-by-side game gun is without peer. Prestige and snob appeal aside, that is why there is a growing cadre of discriminating hunters today who are willing to wait three or more years and pay staggering sums to own the finest game guns money can buy. After hefting a Purdey "best" or a Holland & Holland Royal Grade, one quickly realizes that a thing of beauty is, indeed, a joy forever.

Competing for the attention and affection of royalty and gentry worldwide, the rivalry between London and Birmingham gunmakers has existed for centuries. Each city has its patron saints whose long tradition of gun buildinging is matched by an equally long list of firearms, patents, and designs. Historically, London guns command the higher prices, justified primarily by their exceptional fit and finish. However, Birmingham gunmakers are quick to point out that from a functional standpoint, their guns are a better value for the money.

Throughout the history of the trade in England, famous houses in both cities often jobbed out gun parts such as rough barrels and locks to independent gunmakers. Whether these jobbers resided in London or Birmingham was of little concern to the gunmaker whose name was finally engraved on the barrels. More often than not, especially in today's gun trade, many craftsmen trained by old masters from the prestigious gun houses eventually become self-employed. Contracting their work independently, in many instances back to the very company that taught them their skills, these young masters are changing the traditions in the trade.

Better education has also had a profound effect on the character of England's gun trade. No longer content to labor long hours for paltry pay, wearing a hole in the floor at the bench as did their predecessors, the new generation of gunmakers in London and Birmingham are demanding—and getting—greater compensation for their work.

At present, it appears that a double-gun renaissance is sweeping America, and the high-grade Parkers, Lefevers, Foxes, and L. C. Smiths of yesteryear are commanding sums their creators would never have imagined. The quest for perfection is circular: Once the American hunter discovered that he didn't need $1\frac{1}{4}$-ounce maximum loads and three-shot repeaters to kill upland birds effectively, his natural inclination was to return to the classic side-by-side. Instead of quantity, his search for quality hunting experiences afield had once again led him to an appreciation of quality guns. Such nostalgia, while encouraging, can be carried one step further with the purchase of a modern game gun.

Instead of trying to fit oneself to a turn-of-the-century shotgun whose stock is probably too short and barrels too long, the hunter should research the numerous English, European, and North American gunmakers who can tailor a game gun to fit his physique and personal taste. Sadly enough, of the half-dozen or so gun dealers in the U.S. today who specialize in classic shotguns of older vintage, some are taking undue advantage of a growing number of hunters who desire a quality side-by-side. Capitalizing on eagerness and naiveté, these dealers continue to peddle outrageously priced double guns that belong more in a collector's closet than in an upland covert. "Caveat emptor" is alive and well; many an unsuspecting hunter has been saddled with a "classic" side-by-side ill-suited for work afield, except perhaps for pressing down strands of barbed wire.

Modern production methods, such as diecasting, laser inletting, and cybernetics will unquestionably economize the manufacture of contemporary game guns. They cannot, however, create a more precise game gun design or replace the subtle vitality only skilled hands can instill in wood and steel. The future can only improve the appreciation all hunters should have for the generations of dedicated gunmakers who distilled the classic game gun to its purest form.

What Joseph Manton and colleagues brought to life in their dimly lit, backroom London shops almost two centuries ago lives today because their quest for a truly functional sporting arm was fulfilled. They built a prototype for perfection that compels true firearms craftsmen and artisans to this very day. From muzzleloader to breechloader, only the mechanics have changed; the classic form remains. In an age when everything seems bent on microchip miniaturization, the classic game gun will always require two firm hands for holding and a shoulder for mounting. So long as men hunt, these basic truths will suspend the classic game gun in animation for centuries to come.

In the foreseeable future, as game bird habitat is sacrificed to feed and house a growing world population, reduced bag limits and hunting opportunities will no doubt compel sportsmen to pursue other aspects of the hunt. Logically, the quality of the hunting experience as well as the quality of the firearm the hunter carries afield will command more attention. The added dimension a personally tailored game gun can offer to the wingshooter will help compensate for shorter seasons and fewer birds. After all, much of the joy of owning a custom-fitted and engraved game gun comes during the ten months it spends in the hunter's gun cabinet. To be able to casually pull such a piece from the rack, swing it through imaginary targets on the wall, and feel its built-in quality and balance is one of the things that enable a hunter to endure the passing of seasons. The price of a best-quality game gun is small when compared to the generations of sporting pleasure it will provide.

2

A Fit Gun

When a game bird flushes, all the banter about gunfit, style, and gauge is lost in the flurry of gun mounting, swing, and trigger pull. However, prior to the flush, every bird hunter should research the dynamics of game gun handling before he carries one afield. In England, where a proper gentleman shooter would denounce Queen and Country before peppering a flushed bird in the rump, game guns were developed primarily for shooting driven birds. As such, English stocks have been fashioned with straight, high combs to help compensate for incoming game. High combs place the shooter's eye well above the barrels, causing the gun, when mounted, to shoot high. Upon shouldering such a gun for the first time, most American hunters, accustomed to shorter, less-straight stocks, struggle to find a comfortable fit. Yet, there is a compromise to be struck between the English and American shooting styles that can enhance a hunter's success on shots at flushing birds.

The length of pull (distance between the center of the butt and the front trigger) on most English guns averages ½ to 1½ inches longer than the standard shotguns currently produced by America's gunmakers. Given enough time and determination, it is possible for a hunter to adapt himself to just about anything resembling a stock. Many country boys have become proficient enough with clublike shotguns to outshoot the purist and cast some degree of doubt on all this custom gun fitting business. But for every hunter who has mastered a poorly fitting stock, there are a hundred more who needlessly torture noses, cheekbones, and lips with thumb knuckles and stock combs.

Just as a tailor provides the cure for a man who is tripping over his trousers, the custom gunmaker can remedy many of the shooting ills caused by an unresponsive shooting industry and a lifetime of misinformation about what constitutes proper gunfit. The size of a man's hands, the length of his arms, the set of his shoulders, the length of his neck, and the shape of his cheekbone all contribute to the shouldering of a gun. It should come as no surprise, then, that the average fourteen-inch length of pull fits only an average number of hunters. Ever meet a hunter who considered himself average? Neither have I. There is nothing mysterious about proper gunfit. When correctly fitted, the stock is nothing more than a brace to absorb recoil and hold the shooter's head and eyes on target at all times.

A game gun is no less a personal statement than an automobile or a tweed shooting jacket. The try-gun is the essential first step taken by serious hunters who are searching for a proper gun to take game in the uplands. All the great gunmakers from Parker to Purdey have extolled the virtues of the try-gun.

With its adjustable settings, the try-gun can be shaped to conform to one's physique, compensating for important variables factory guns cannot. Length of pull not only depends on a man's arm length, but also on the bone and muscle structure of his upper shoulder. Prostheses for amputated extremities are not fitted carelessly, because they must interact almost involuntarily with body movement; the game gun stock must perform similarly if any consistency or competence is to be realized by the hunter. It is the hunter's visual crutch and should respond involuntarily as well.

Unfortunately, gun fitting can be as confusing as it can be enlightening. Go to a half-dozen different gunmakers in England or elsewhere, and you are likely to get that many different gunfit dimensions. However, most individuals who can afford a custom-fitted

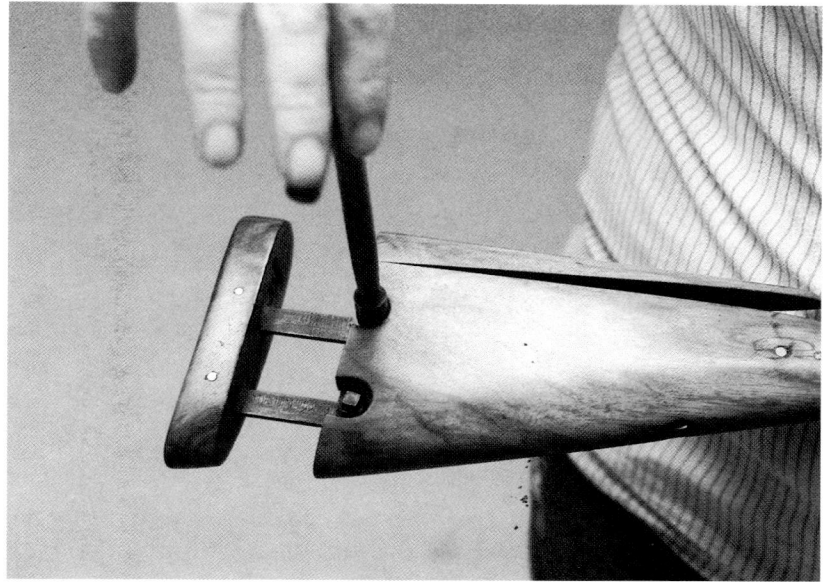

shotgun take their shooting seriously, and usually have more gunning experience than the average hunter. In this regard, there is really no substitute for common sense and remembered experiences afield.

It's best to rely on your intuition and communicate your thoughts to the gun fitter. Tell him the kind of hunting conditions you will be encountering in your pet coverts; let him know the range of temperatures from beginning to end of your hunting season; inform him of the amount of clothing you will wear afield. In short, try to separate some of the sales sizzle from the steak, and arrive at a fit that is comfortable and functional.

My first formal gun fitting took place in an English gunmaker's dank, tool-strewn shop. The old gunmaker was ruddy complected and had an elfin quality about him. He quietly sized me up, his eyes darting about my anatomy like a cannibal sizing up a missionary. His silver hair belied his cunning wit and spry movements as he adjusted the eighty-year-old try-gun to fit my six-foot, four-inch frame. He quipped about my Yankee arms, attributing their thirty-six-inch length to good nutrition and an American lust for bigger and better things.

Before placing the multi-jointed gun in my hands, he inchwormed a grease-stained tape measure down my outstretched left arm and across my shoulders. He deftly measured the circumference of my chest, neck, and left hand with the speed of a Manhattan tailor. A few quick adjustments with the T-wrench at the wrist of the stock gave him the desired pitch and bend ("cast"). He fussed with the gun's length of pull, carefully tapping out the adjustable butt section like a grocer fine-tuning the weights on a meat scale. All the while, he quizzed me about the types of upland birds I hunted, whether I would be shooting "walk-up" or "driven birds," and what kind of weather conditions I would encounter on my favorite hunting grounds.

With initial adjustments made, the old gunmaker opened the try-gun to reassure me that it was not loaded, then handed me the hand-rubbed relic. Immediately, I was surprised at how well balanced the odd-looking gun felt. To gain height advantage, the gunmaker pulled out a small step stool from under his bench. Standing on the stool a few yards away, he asked me to mount the gun as swiftly as possible. He instructed me to keep both eyes open and use his right eye for my point of aim. Even though the try-gun was empty, I felt uneasy about pointing it at the gunmaker.

Accustomed to stocks considerably shorter in length, my first mounting attempt hooked the butt of the try-gun in my armpit. Without so much as a ho-hum or chortle, the gunmaker stoically requested that I try again. My second effort was successful, but before I could ask what he thought, he abruptly declared "too much bend," and took the gun to make another series of adjustments. "By the way," the gunmaker said as he cranked on the stock, "you Yanks may bloody

Makers of fine English Quality Shotguns

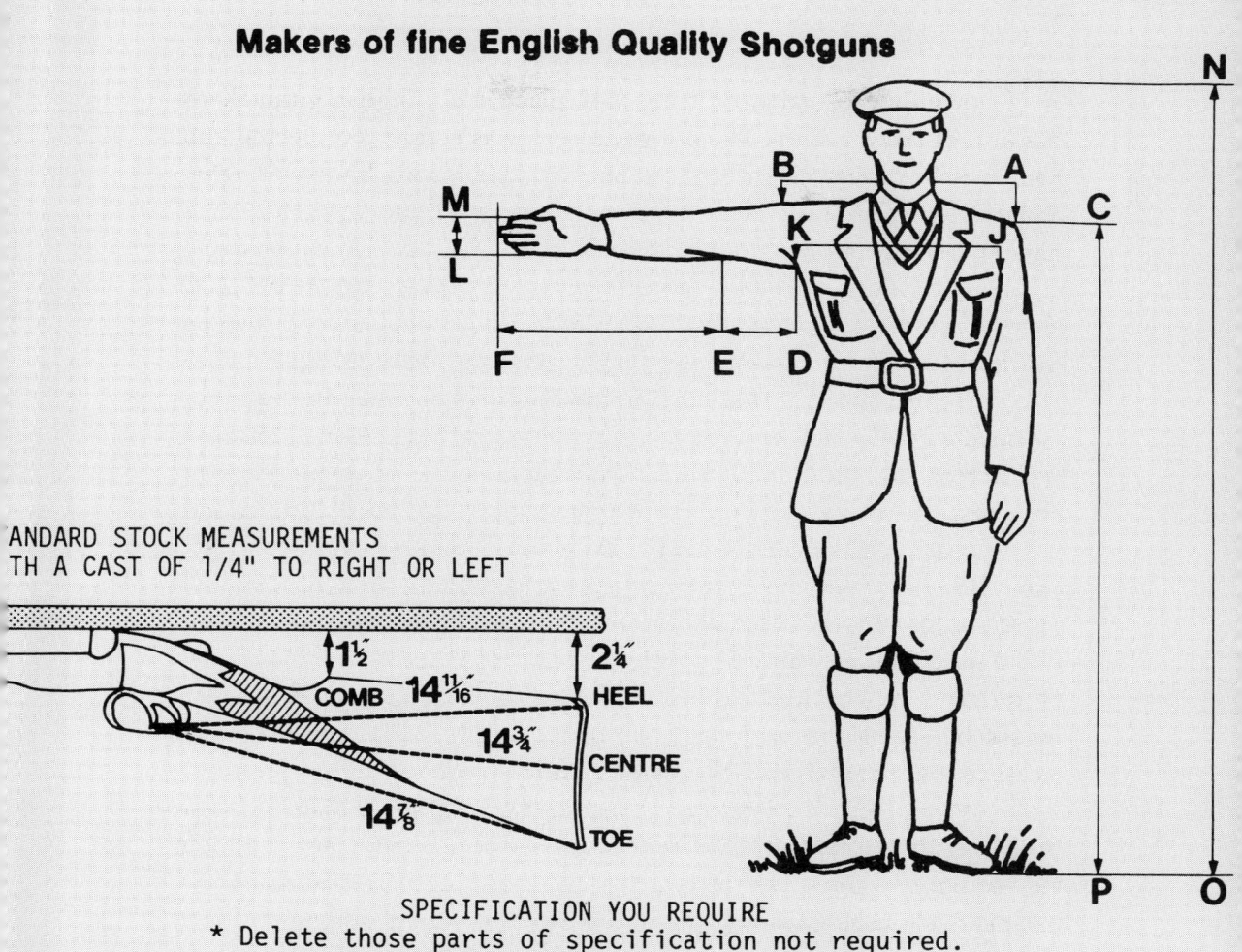

STANDARD STOCK MEASUREMENTS
WITH A CAST OF 1/4" TO RIGHT OR LEFT

- COMB: 1½"
- HEEL: 2¼"
- 14 11/16" (COMB)
- 14 ¾" (CENTRE)
- 14 ⅞" (TOE)

SPECIFICATION YOU REQUIRE
* Delete those parts of specification not required.

SIZE OF BORE	12	16	20	28	
LENGTH OF BARREL	25	26	27	28	30
TYPE OF CHOKE	IMP CYL	¼	½	¾	FULL
SIZE OF CHAMBER	2½	2¾		LH	

IMP CYL	¼	½	¾	FULL
RH				

CAST
BEND

* [STRAIGHT] or [HALF PISTOL] HAND STOCK
* OTHER EXTRAS

YOU SHOOT WITH:

A. BOTH EYES OPEN?
B. ONE EYE CLOSED?
IF 'B' WHICH IS CLOSED? | LEFT | RIGHT |
IF 'A' WHICH IS MASTER EYE? | LEFT | RIGHT |

DO YOU SHOOT FROM THE | LEFT |
                       | RIGHT | SHOULDER?

SUPPLEMENTARY MEASUREMENTS

HEIGHT	O - N	INS
"	P - C	"
WIDTH	A - B	"
"	J - K	"
LENGTH	E - D	"
"	F - D	"
WIDTH	M - L	"
WEIGHT		LBS
* MAN		
* WOMAN		

17

well know how to squeeze off a rifle, but you could all use a few lessons in proper shotgun mounting."

"How's that?" I asked, somewhat defensively. He went on to explain that the English use a three-step method that assures precise gun mounting, pointing, and follow-through. "Kind of a 'ready,' 'set,' 'go!' procedure," he said, demonstrating the three positions. The "ready" position is assumed with the gun's barrels angled up, the buttstock at the hip, and the trigger finger alongside the trigger guard. On "set," the gun is brought up to shoulder level with the buttstock tucked lightly under the armpit and the muzzles tracking the moving target. An all-or-nothing commitment, "go!" is the instinctive command given by the brain to fire the gun at the target the instant the buttstock makes contact with the shoulder pocket.

In order to establish proper lead, the body must begin moving to intercept the target as the gun is being mounted to the shoulder. He explained that if the gun was swiftly mounted from waist level, the possibility of shooting over or under the target would be increased. The three-step method ensures a more accurate mount.

Hesitant at first, I practiced the three-part procedure for a few minutes until I was mounting the gun smoothly. Satisfied with my progress, the gunmaker resumed the gun fitting session. On the fifth trip to the shoulder, and after a few intermittent adjustments to the try-gun, my master fitter said the dimensions were about right, but a visit to the shooting range would be required to make the final adjustments.

On the way to the shooting grounds, I began to wonder what I had let myself in for. An experienced hunter, I thought I was well versed on the handling dynamics of upland bird guns. My British gunmaker was already shooting holes in some of my pet theories, but I was determined to carry this gun fitting experience to its conclusion, in spite of my deflated ego.

The shooting grounds were as manicured as a well-kept golf course. The almost clinical surroundings were a little intimidating to a country boy who was used to a more rustic shooting environment.

The gunmaker pointed to a large target backdrop some fifty yards downrange. Spaced intermittently along the metal target-board

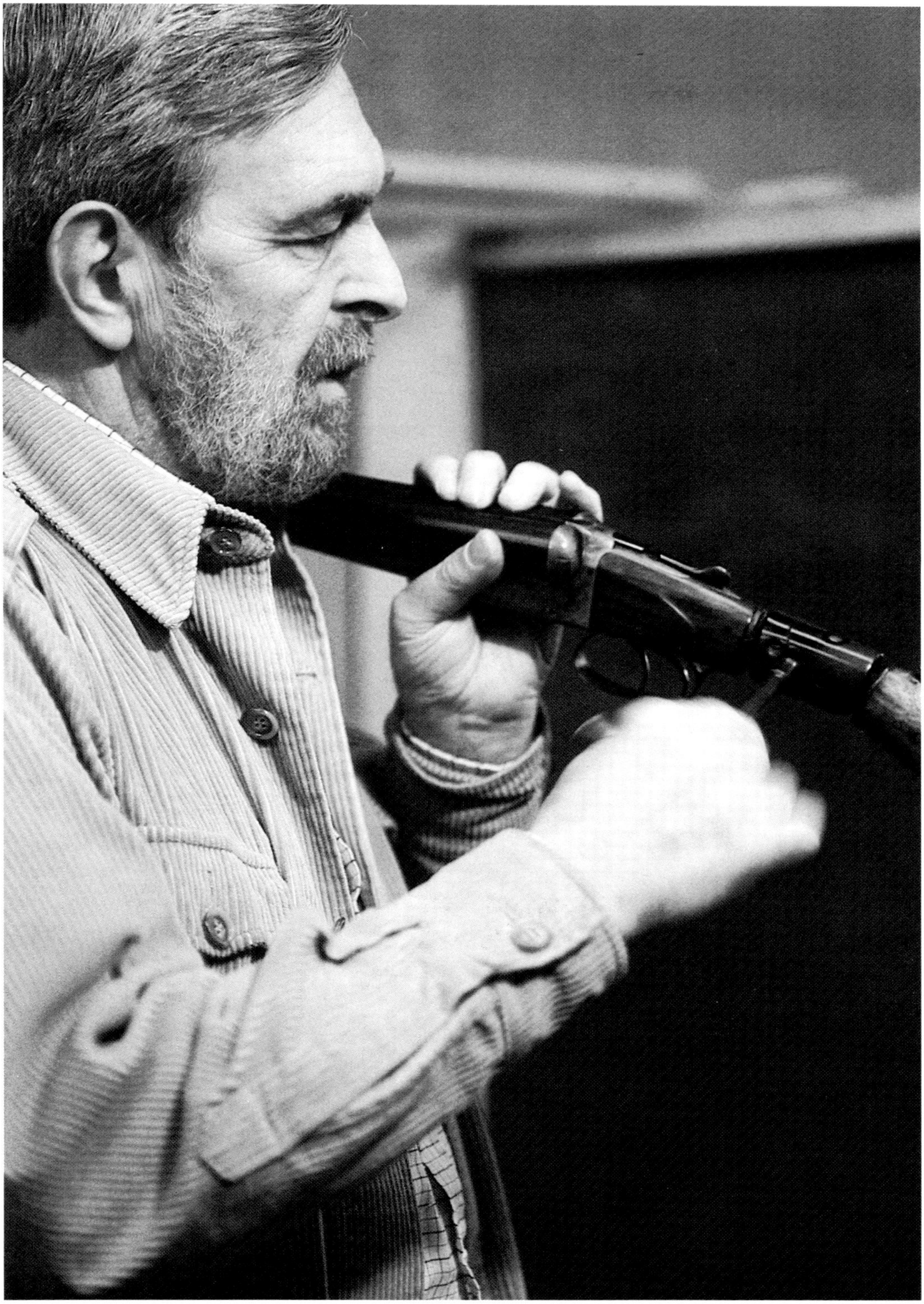

were outlines of six partridge-sized birds in flight. At this point, I was introduced to a distinguished-looking shooting instructor. He discussed the try-gun measurements with the gunmaker, then guided me to a predetermined shooting position about twenty-five yards from the target board. In matter-of-fact fashion and proper King's English, the instructor detailed the final, though crucial, gun fitting procedure.

The try-gun, he explained, was choked improved-cylinder in the right barrel and regulated for $1\frac{1}{16}$ ounces of shot. The instructor handed me an Eley target load from his leather shooting bag and told me to instinctively mount the gun, concentrating only on the target as I fired. My first shot raised a puff of paint a foot and a half above and to the right of the target.

The instructor, who was peering intensely over my shoulder, took the try-gun, lowered its comb, and adjusted the stock's cast. I reloaded the gun, brought it to my shoulder, and fired at the second target. The pattern was still high but well centered over the target. A quick adjustment to the comb put my third shot on the mark. I

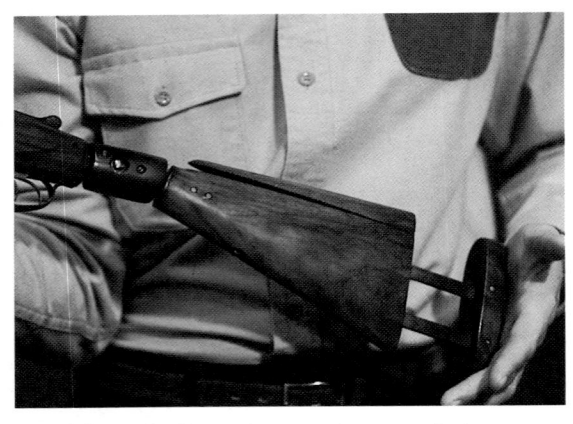

Crucial stock dimensions such as comb drop, length of pull, cast, and pitch are all a part of a try-gun's repertoire. Such a gun can transform an "average" shooter into the unique individual he is.

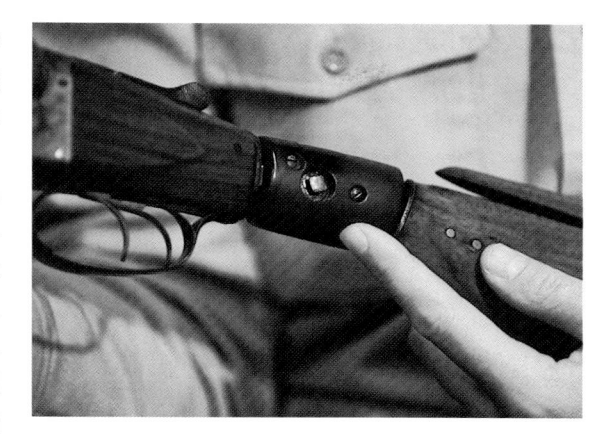

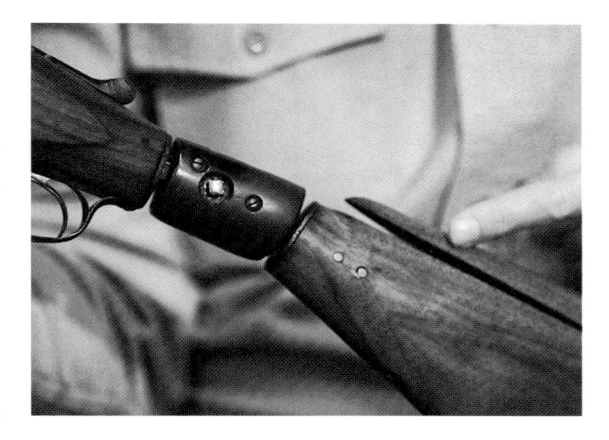

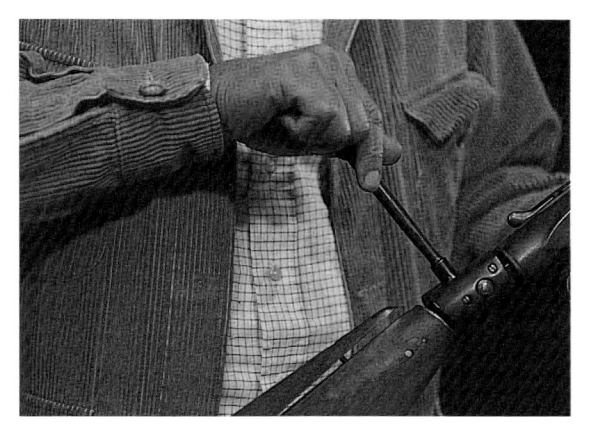

fired twice more to make sure that I was mounting and pointing the gun properly.

On the clay-bird course later that afternoon, I shot targets at every conceivable angle. After each hit or miss, the instructor would evaluate my form and footwork. Probably because we start shooting at a young age when recoil is a problem, American shooters tend to take a wider stance than is necessary, causing them to drop their shoulders on crossing targets. Once I adopted a narrower stance which allowed me to shift my weight more naturally, I began to powder targets consistently.

The instructor was very thorough and professional. He minced few words in describing the theoretical and practical aspects of gunfit and wingshooting form. Unlike American trap and skeet, the walk-up claybird course I shot that day offered a challenging array of crossing targets, low going-away shots, and high overheads. Such hunter's clay courses are gaining popularity across America (the Orvis grounds in Houston are a fine example). They are excellent places for honing wingshooting skills before, during, and after the hunting season.

The British have always had a penchant for long, straight stocks. I was surprised how well I handled and shot the longer-than-normal length of pull on the old try-gun. Before wishing me Godspeed and good shooting, the instructor translated the try-gun dimensions onto parchment: length of pull—15½ inches; drop at comb—1½ inches; drop at heel—2 inches and a ⅛-inch cast-on (I'm a lefthanded shooter, so my "cast-on" is really "cast-off"—away from my face). The instructor mentioned that such statistics are not etched in granite, and that as I aged they would probably require some modification. Bone structure and musculature change with age, requiring periodic adjustment of the stock, usually more drop and more cast.

In such early gun fitting experiences, I was wide-eyed putty in the hands of stockmakers, and I was frequently measured up with that long, 15- to 15½-inch pull length that felt good in the gunshop but became a contortionist's nightmare during unexpected flushes in the field. Experimentation and feedback with a gun fitter since those early days eventually led me to a maximum pull length of 14¾ inches for straight-grip guns and 14½ inches for those with pistol grips. A simple rule of thumb to follow is to try to adapt your style to a longer, straighter stock. Such a stock will tend to stop head-lifting; a long stock makes a shooter subconsciously pull "into the gun," thus keeping his head down. If too long, it can always be gradually reduced in length and drop until fit and performance become one.

Climate and clothing must always be considered during any try-gun fitting. Obviously, a stock measured for a shooter in a short-sleeved shirt will be too long come hunting season when he sports a down vest and shooting jacket. The try-gun is no substitute for common sense, and most knowledgeable gun fitters will be quick to ask what types of shooting conditions the hunter will encounter and adjust the gun accordingly. Usually a quarter- to half-inch reduction in length of pull is sufficient compensation for hunting clothes.

A Fit Gun

The upland hunter who pursues grouse, woodcock, and quail through dense cover soon discovers that quick and accurate gun mounting is the key to bringing down game. Consistently good wingshots usually swing guns that fit. Such guns enable the shooter to position his cheek on the same spot on the stock each time the gun is mounted, thus assuring a proper sight picture and precise gun pointing.

Because of fast-departing game, many hunters feel they must quickly slide the buttstock to their shoulder, figuring, no doubt, that the shortest distance between two points is a straight line. What often happens is that the buttstock gets impeded by or caught in the hunter's clothing on its way to the shoulder. Then, instead of bringing the stock up to the cheek, the shooter forces his head down to accommodate the improperly fitted stock, making for an awkward shot at best.

The English "forward thrust" method of gun mounting I learned, along with a properly fitted gun, achieves two important objectives: it creates a consistent shoulder pocket for gun mounting, and it places the buttstock in this pocket unencumbered by the shooter's clothing.

By its very structure, the English game gun forces the shooter's leading hand to become more than a barrel rest during the process of mounting and shooting. This hand must push the gun out from the body, up toward the target, and back into the shoulder pocket in one fluid motion. The grip hand, in turn, merely follows the leading hand throughout the thrust-forward procedure. The leading hand should also lead the swing of the gun and upper body through the target upon firing. Once mastered, this thrust-forward gun-mounting method becomes as natural as pointing your finger.

Once a comfortable length of pull has been achieved, the next critical factor in proper game gun fitting involves the drop at the comb nose. Because the comb, as a cheek rest, aligns the sight plane of the barrels with the eyes, it must be of proper height and shape. A low, thinly tapered comb can punish the shooter unmercifully. Such combs are often encountered on old, turn-of-the-century double guns.

During this period, hunters were taught to keep their heads almost totally erect while shooting. Adding insult to injury, a stock of this vintage usually had an excessive drop at the heel (3–3½ inches) which was tolerable for gentle straightaway shots but difficult to control on the sharp, quartering targets upland birds often provide. Modern game gun stocks, as a rule, are fitted with thicker, more rounded combs and with a drop at the heel seldom exceeding 2½ inches, unless the shooter has a long neck and sloping shoulders.

I learned much of this the hard way while on an Iowa pheasant hunt with a rangy red setter and an old Parker 16-gauge, circa 1902. With a makeshift shoulder pad beneath my shooting vest to compensate for the short stock, and with proper feelings of nostalgia for the old gun, I accounted for my fair share of wild-flushing roosters. Most birds obliged the crooked-stocked little Parker by flushing straightaway and were taken in matter-of-fact fashion.

However, toward the end of the hunt, my setter stumbled over a cockbird forty yards immediately to my right. It towered, then angled sharply in front of me. I tracked, mounted, covered, and fired in one swift motion. Such right-to-left shots humble most southpaw hunters, but I did myself proud and cleanly folded the bird. I would have smugly tucked the pheasant in my game bag, had I not removed all the sensation from my lower lip and upper cheekbone. Because of the ill-fitted stock, I had lifted my head off the comb to follow the bird. The short stock and recoil rudely introduced thumb to lip and comb to cheek. When my hunting partners offered their congratulations, all I could do was motion to them with a feeble "thumbs-up" gesture.

That particular gun and shot taught me a great deal about stock fit. I have relegated that engaging piece of American history to a corner of my gun cabinet where I occasionally pull it out, reminisce about the good old days, and carefully set it back in its proper place of retirement.

Considering the dynamics of recoil, it is interesting to note that the barrel sequence on some English side-by-sides is determined by the shooter's handedness, right or left. The barrel sequence in American double guns has always been right barrel first (in either double-trigger or single-trigger guns); some English shooters prefer just the opposite arrangement. Many right-handed shooters in England contend that to minimize felt recoil and keep the gun properly aligned for a quick second shot, the left barrel should be fired first because it recoils more directly in line with the shoulder. Recoil from the right barrel has a tendency to pull the gun away from the shoulder and face of a right-handed shooter. It would follow, then, that southpaw shooters should feel right at home with the standard right-left barrel sequence. It makes you wonder if there is anything in shotgunning and gunmaking the British have overlooked.

Once a comfortable drop at comb and heel have been determined, another important factor to consider is what degree of cast the gun should have. Referred to as "cast-off" to right-handed shooters and "cast-on" to lefties, the stock is bent laterally left or right in increments anywhere from $\frac{1}{8}$- to $\frac{1}{2}$-inch or more. On custom guns, the angle of cast in the stock is built-in from the receiver to butt. A gunstock's cast can be altered by wrapping the wrist (or "hand") of the stock with a burlap-like material (old-timers in the trade still use horsetail) and then saturating it with linseed oil which has been heated almost to the point of combustion. The hot oil is combined with steady pressure from a special stock-bending jig, or the stockmaker's educated hip, until the desired amount of cast is achieved.

Some may wonder why a reasonable neutral (no cast) stock couldn't do away with all this "casting" about. For some shooters, a neutral stock is perfectly adequate, but anatomy dictates proper gunfit. Good game gun makers strive to eliminate as many obstacles to instinctive gun mounting as possible to let the hunter concentrate on his target instead of trying to adjust to a poorly fitted stock.

As critical as length of pull, drop, and cast dimensions are to the traditional method of gun fitting, many in the British gun trade give little, if any, consideration to the pitch of a shotgun. Pitch or "pitch down" is measured by standing the shotgun upright on the floor and placing the heel of the stock and receiver breech against a perpendicular wall or door. This procedure angles the barrels away from the vertical axis, thus determining the amount of pitch built into the gun. Pitch dimensions will vary from gun to gun depending on barrel length and drop of the stock. Pitch usually falls between 1½ and 2½ inches on guns with twenty-eight-inch barrels.

A shotgun with a great deal of stock drop and pitch will have a tendency to shoot lower than a gun fitted with a straighter stock and less pitch. As such, most English game guns with their minimal drop dimensions at the comb and heel have very little pitch at the barrels; some may even have zero pitch. This gives the barrels a decided upward influence when the gun is mounted, offering the shooter a slight built-in lead for flushing and incoming game birds. Many of the old Parkers, Foxes, Lefevers, and such were built with considerable drop and pitch, making them well suited for ground-running game such as rabbits, foxes, and poachers.

The main factor affecting a shotgun's pitch is the angle at which the buttstock is cut from heel to toe. If the angle of the cut favors the heel of the stock, the gun will have a tendency to point low. When the angle favors the toe of the stock, the shotgun will have an inclination to shoot high. However, consideration must again be given to the anatomy of the shooter. A barrel-chested, round-shouldered shooter, for example, will handle pitch with less difficulty than someone of slighter build. Conversely, the shooter with average shoulder muscles will normally cozy up nicely to a shotgun having less pitch.

A gun's apparent pitch can, to a degree, be changed by the shooter without making any physical alterations to the gun. The shooter can compensate for a gun with a great deal of pitch by simply extending his leading hand down the barrels. This will raise the point of aim slightly, making the shotgun somewhat more suitable for rising birds. Conversely, the shooter can also alleviate the high-shooting tendencies of a gun with very little pitch by placing his leading hand closer to the action body. Such hand placement tends to drop the barrels' point of aim for the hunter who prefers to shoot rising birds without any built-in lead.

Another subtle refinement which can add to the comfort and precision of one's shooting is the angle of twist from the heel to toe on the buttstock. Depending on the shape of the shoulder pocket created when you raise your arm into shooting position, the amount of heel-toe twist on the stock can be adjusted accordingly to ensure consistent alignment of the gun during mounting. The anatomy of the shooter's shoulder and upper chest must be given careful consideration by the stockfitter as well. Ideally, stock measurements should be taken on the shooting range with a try-gun that can be fired. Using at first a stationary target twenty-five to forty yards downrange, the hunter should instinctively mount and fire the try-gun after each adjustment is made until its pattern is centering on the target or as desired.

Each step in this procedure should also be closely supervised by a capable shooting instructor and try-gun fitter. If any aspect of the shotgun manufacture is carried to an extreme, it should be the stockfitting procedure. Once comfortable dimensions have been achieved, a round or two of sporting clays will help refine the final fit.

Opinions on what style and gauge constitute a fit gun for upland hunting are legion. Many English shotgunners prefer a sidelock 12-gauge side-by-side, while a growing number of American sportsmen tend to lean toward the over-under 20-gauge.

The elegance of the sidelock side-by-side is difficult to ignore, just as the utility of a boxlock over-under is tough to dispute, but I believe there exists a gauge-style combination that both logic and sentiment support as the ideal game gun: the 16-gauge side-by-side.

All but abandoned by U.S. firearms manufacturers and gun writers, the 16 side-by-side affords a sleekness of design and effectiveness of gauge that delivers an ounce of birdshot more efficiently than either the 12 or 20. Within normal shooting ranges, few upland bird hunting situations require more than an ounce of shot; the 16-gauge with $2\frac{3}{4}$-inch chambers was designed specifically for one-ounce loads. Shot charge in relation to bore diameter for the 16-gauge one-ounce load is excellent. Such "square loads" minimize shot deformation from bore scrub and take full advantage of properly choked barrels. Quail hunters in the southern United States have long heralded the virtues of the 16-gauge side-by-side, and many a woodcock and grouse has been brought to dog by the open-choked, twin tubes of the 16. Loaded with $2\frac{1}{2}$ dram-equivalent of powder, the one-ounce 16-gauge shotshell is pleasant to shoot and deadly effective on upland birds. Dedicated 16-gauge shooters report less apparent lead is necessary on crossing birds with this bore, proof of a fast, efficient load with little stringing.

At present, Europe remains the last bastion of the 16-gauge game gun. Belgians, Frenchmen, and Spaniards are still fond of its eye-pleasing grace and portability. Weighing from five pounds, eleven ounces to six pounds, seven ounces, the 16 is a delight to carry in the field and does not exhibit the toyness of a 20, nor the bulk of a 12-gauge. Built in boxlock or sidelock (the preference of the purist), the much ignored 16-gauge can provide the hunter with a game gun fit for most upland shooting conditions. And while certain shotgun aficionados may claim the ounce of shot crammed into their superlight 28-gauges will equal the 16's performance, they need only examine their sore cheekbones, tender shoulders, and the pattern board to disprove the logic of their choice. For the hunter who is bored with the firearm industry's hyperbole concerning the endless feats of the three-inch magnum 20-gauge, and just a little tired of lugging an overweight 12 over hill and dale, a 16-gauge double is a most fit game gun for North American shooting.

The debate among side-by-side enthusiasts concerning the merits of boxlock versus sidelock game guns has raged for nearly a hundred years. Aside from notable variations in lock (firing) mechanisms, there is really very little difference between the two styles.

While the author's preference lies with the esthetically pleasing lines of a sidelock, the boxlock is actually an advance in game gun design. Sidelocks merely internalize the rabbit-ear hammers of muzzleloading side-by-sides, while boxlocks were a design refinement that simplified the lock mechanism for trouble-free service in game fields far from gunsmiths' shops. Boxlocks are rugged, down-to-earth performers, while their sidelock counterparts tend to be somewhat more blue-blooded and prone to lavish embellishment. As far as performance afield is concerned, either style will provide the hunter with two certain shots and a choice of chokes. The real debate arises when the virtues of the side-by-side are matched against those of other styles of shotguns.

A Fit Gun

Long before the Industrial Age and automation ushered in repeating sporting arms, the side-by-side smoothbore had proved its effectiveness on wild game. Such care and attention was lavished on the better makes of double guns produced in both England and the United States around the turn of the century that an aura of snobbery lingers over the side-by-side to this day.

The inherent handling qualities of a best-quality game gun are often overlooked by gun writers who are convinced that the so-called "single sighting plane," found on repeaters and over-unders ensures better performance afield. The truth is, all guns have only one sighting plane. And while the narrowness of single or stacked barrels might offer a great advantage to the rifleman who aims his firearm, it is of little significance to the upland hunter who must instinctively mount and point his shotgun. There are, of course, exceptions, such as pass-shooting waterfowl. But for upland bird work, the natural pointing characteristics of a properly built side-by-side are a considerable asset.

In "groove" games like today's trap and skeet, where ponderous and unbalanced shotguns are already to the shoulder, a narrow sighting plane can be justified. Upland game guns, however, are pointed—not aimed—and no heavyweight pump or autoloader, regardless of how bastardized to the contrary, will outpoint a well-balanced side-by-side. In fact, properly ribbed and tapered game gun barrels have a definite funneling effect on the vision, especially for those who shoot with both eyes open. Any hunter who consciously sees the rib or bead on his gun when shooting game birds is looking at the wrong thing. The eyes should be transfixed on the target alone.

The side-by-side has more going for it than a long tradition of royal appointments and literary accounts of its classic accomplishments afield. Its built-in lateral stability facilitates precise pointing, reducing the shooter's tendency to cant (twist) a gun left or right as often occurs with over-under doubles. Loading and unloading the side-by-side is simplified by its smaller angle of opening and low center of gravity. The shapely bottom contours of its receiver allow comfortable carrying afield as well.

A fit game gun, then, embodies many unrelated aspects that are integrated into a functional whole. Captivating engraving, smoothly struck barrels, and crisp ejectors all contribute to the total gun, but are superfluous if the gunstock does not fit the shooter. In quality game guns, the shotgun is built around the stock, not the stock around the gun. Gauge, style, and embellishment are insignificant unless the superstructure of the stock is fitted properly to the shooter. Gunfit is as personal as one's signature; it stands to reason that success afield will come to those who come to grips with a custom-fitted stock.

Visions come to those who dream, and there are no greater dreamers than those who pursue wild game birds. Dream guns exist in the minds of all serious game gunners. Gauges, choke combinations, barrel lengths, rib configurations, stock grips, and other optional features all figure into the final analysis of the hunter's perfect gun.

The author's lingering vision is a 16-gauge sidelock game gun with straight grip, double triggers, and two sets of $27\frac{1}{2}$-inch barrels, choked cylinder/improved-cylinder in the first set, improved-cylinder/improved-modified in the second set. The esthetically appealing 16 handles an ounce of birdshot like no other gauge, and the choke combinations span the gamut of cover conditions from tight thickets to sprawling grain fields. It is a fit game gun in every sense of the word.

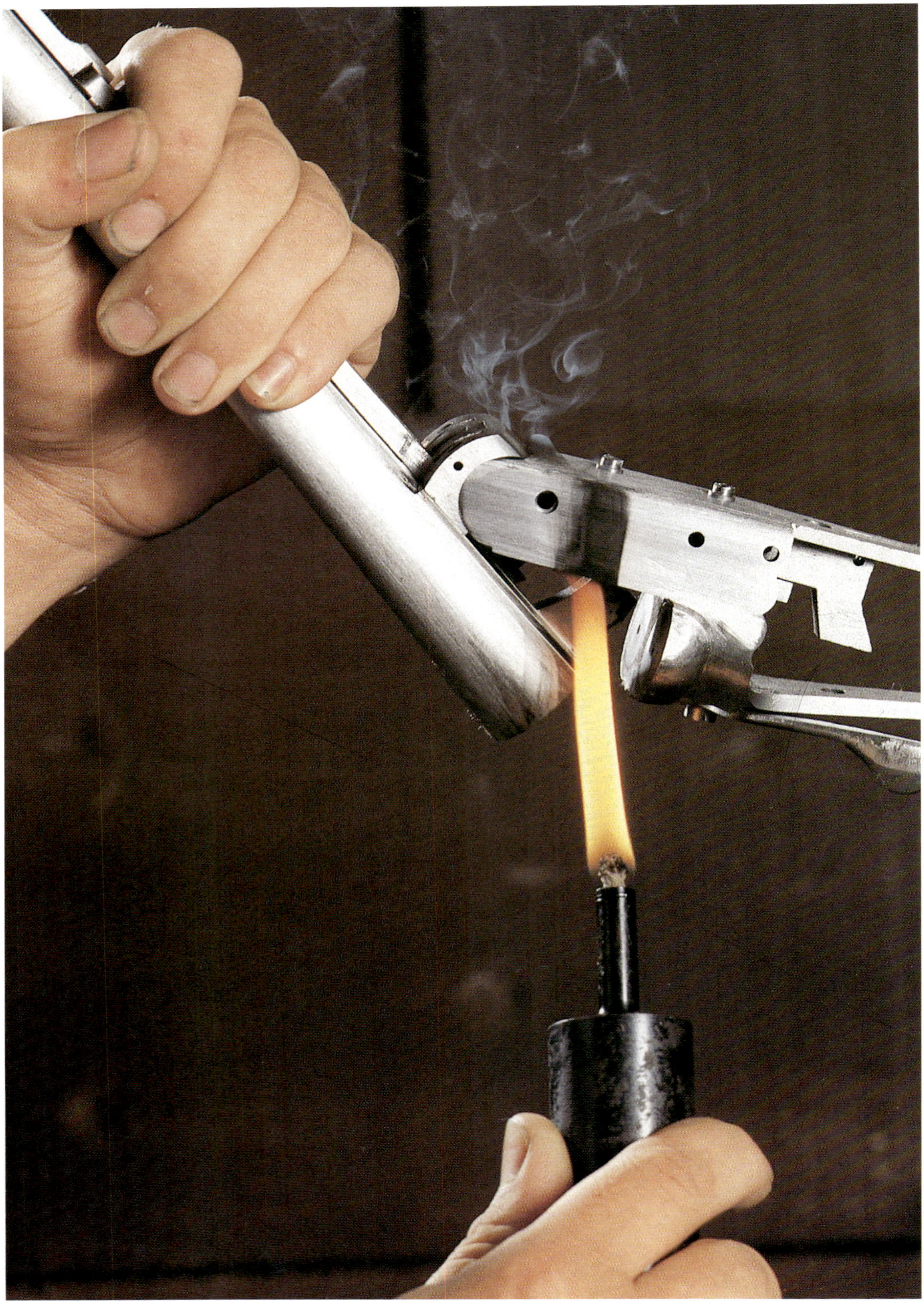

3

METAL TO METAL

From primitive smelters to sophisticated furnaces, man continues to advance technology to transform crude ore into high-quality steel. Nowhere is steel fashioned and fondled with more care than in the gun trade. For centuries gunmakers in England, France, Spain, Italy, Germany, and other countries have refined their techniques and tools to take advantage of the malleability and durability of shooting steel. Like the breeding of fine horseflesh, gunmetal demands selective alloying and proper handling before it can be shaped into high-class sporting arms.

Traditional game guns have many generations of shooting pleasure built into them. Shaped by hand from rough steel forgings, the metal on a "best" gun receives hundreds of hours of file work before final tolerances are achieved. Sculpted with hammer and steel chisel in much the same fashion an artist brings form to marble, each rough forging, whether barrel, receiver, or lockplate, is treated to a progressive assortment of the action filer's tools. From initial hammer and chisel shaping to final casehardening, every metal part undergoes a transformation that rivals the precision of fine machine work. The subtle interplay between the artisan's hand file and forged metal creates a form that functions with a dynamic smoothness and feel that machines alone cannot duplicate.

BARRELMAKING

Because of the forgiving nature of a shotgun's dispersing pattern, many may suspect that it really isn't all that important to produce truly accurate shotgun barrels. Like precision drilled and button-rifled rifle barrels, great care must also be taken in every phase of manufacture to create shotgun barrels that center their patterns at forty yards. The process by which the gunmaker achieves straight-shooting barrels is called the "truing operation." It begins with rough tubes that have been carefully reamed for true bores (gauges) and ends with externally contoured and tapered barrels that balance the gun's action and stock. Periodically throughout the process, barrel concentricity is checked with various ring gauges, with any imperfections hand-reamed and lapped into acceptable tolerances. Barrel exteriors are then carefully struck down by hand to ensure uniform wall thickness and taper. Barrels started and finished in this manner require less regulating ("Englishing") to deliver proper side-by-side accuracy at the patterning board.

Producing and regulating side-by-side barrels is as much an art as it is a science. Machine and craftsman work together to guarantee durability and accuracy in the horizontal tubes of the game gun. Aside from a few basic cuts made in the receiver forging, fabrication of the barrels requires the lion's share of machining. English barrels are crafted from billets of pressed fluid steel with 3 percent to 12 percent nickel content. Barrel blanks are usually no longer than thirty-one inches and are classified into three general categories: 1) chopper lump—barrels machined with an integral lug that becomes an underlug for bolting; 2) dovetail—barrels machined with a dovetail notch to accept a correspondingly independent lug;

3) monoblock—barrels machined into smooth sleeves for insertion into a one-piece breechblock.

Classic among the three in the English gun trade is the chopper lump configuration. It is also a very strong and dependable system for barrel joining and bolting. Not without some difficulty, a straight hole is rough-bored through each barrel forging. By placing his hand on the outside of the barrel, an experienced barrelmaker can feel the progress of the bit as it drills down the tube. Differing bit sizes are introduced until all the irregularities are removed from the bore. Enough steel must be left at this juncture to compensate for the external striking, internal reaming, lapping, and choke adjustment which will follow.

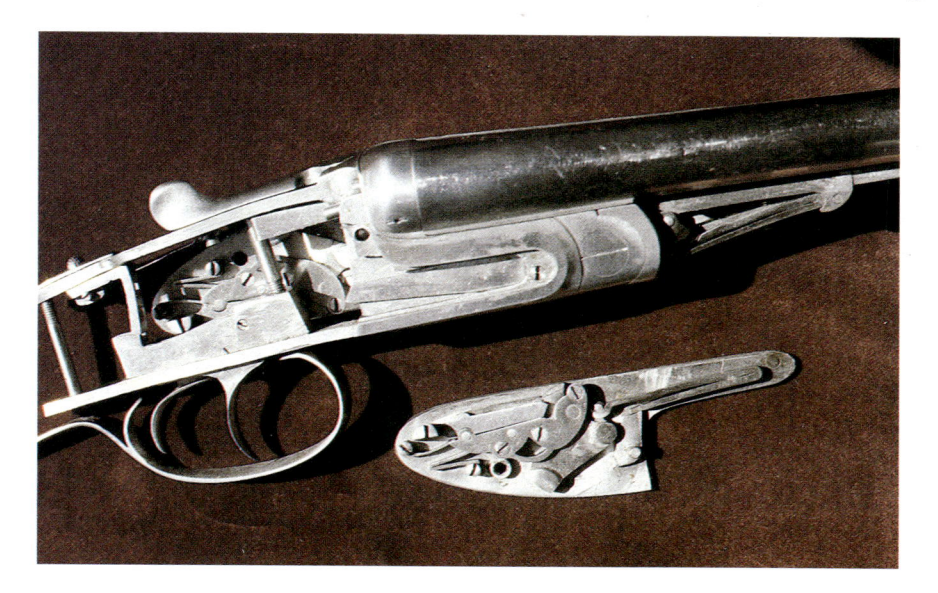

"Spill boring" was the most popular method used in the gun trade to bore the softer Damascus steel tubes as well as early fluid steel barrels. By today's high-tech standards, the spill-boring procedure seems quite crude. But as with all of man's inventions, it had a peculiar personality that required a fine touch to obtain a properly bored set of barrels. The spill-boring apparatus consisted of a ten-inch length of steel about $3/8$-inch square, a quarter-round piece of wood, and a paper shim between the wood and steel bit. This boring unit was then forged onto a steel rod and forced down the bore of the barrel at about forty revolutions per minute. Lubricated with Russian tallow, the primitive bit chirped loudly as it progressed down the bore. By this loud squeaking sound alone, the knowledgeable gunmaker could determine if the barrels were being bored true or if a rip in the barrel steel had developed.

Though the principle remains the same, modern boring machines are infinitely faster and their precision is no longer dependent on a pair of trained ears. Uniform barrel concentricity and thickness must be maintained throughout, because the barrels are individually tapered to properly balance with the dimensions and specifications laid down for the gun.

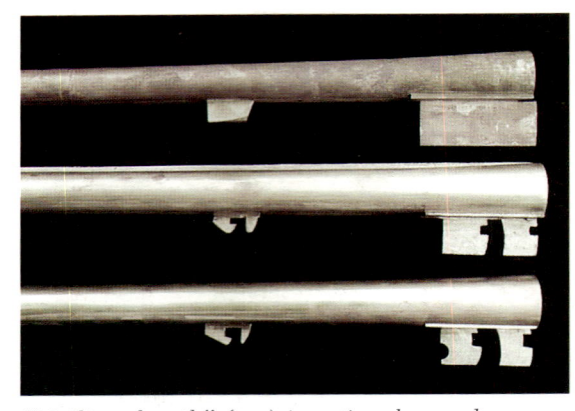

"Nailing the rib" (top) is a time-honored practice among old-world gunmakers. With the aid of milling machines, lampblack, and an assortment of hand files, the gunmaker fashions the fore-end loop and barrel lumps (bottom).

The most critical factor in barrelmaking is the grain structure of the steel being used. Barrel steel must be hammer-forged to align the grain and enable it to remain resilient to the constant expansion and contraction it undergoes during firing.

Gunbarrel steel, from high-grade Damascus to Sir Joseph Whitworth's pressed fluid steel, has always been in demand by the

Damascus barrels and those shot out of proof can be sleeved to restore shootability (top). In various stages of completion, these barrels (bottom) will be hand-fitted and finished to balance the gauge, the gun, and the desired load.

trade and, in years gone by, found its way there in some very unusual ways. A popular pastime of many peasants living in and around Birmingham and London during the late nineteenth and early twentieth centuries was the collection of horseshoe tacks. The scavenged metal was eagerly sought by barrelmakers in the gun trade who felt that its unique properties made superior Damascus gunbarrels.

Apparently, the hammering of horse hooves altered the grain structure of steel tacks in such a way that when the metal blades were welded around a barrel mandrel by the gunmaker, the barrel became stronger and more resistant to wear.

As testimony to the validity of such a tale, some of these very Damascus barrels have received nitro proofs for very light field loads. Vintage Damascus guns should really be appreciated more for their historical significance to the development of the modern game gun and never shot unless fitted with properly sleeved barrels. The English pioneered the method for converting Damascus-tubed guns into solid shooters by cutting off the old barrels about three inches from the breech and countersinking steel sleeve tubes into the breechlock. Properly installed, sleeved barrels can transform otherwise useless doubles into safe and solid performers.

"Thickness of smoke" is the universal tenet of the traditional gun trade.

Worked on as a pair, but still unjoined, fluid steel barrels are stress relieved and given to a barrel filer, who removes the external machining marks in a process known as "barrel striking." Using progressively finer hand files, the British craftsman takes long, smooth strokes from breech to muzzle until exterior blemishes and "camelbacks" are removed from the barrels. At this point, the barrels are checked for straightness by holding the bores up to a light source and inspecting the light rings. Should any crookedness be detected, a few knowing taps of a mallet against the affected barrel-wall will bring it back into correct alignment. The barrels, usually having forty points of choke (full choke), are then final machine-bored.

Still "in the white" (unblued), the barrel lumps are then brazed, not silver soldered, three inches up the barrels from the breech end. The lumps on both barrels are then machined and filed

Smoking the bearing surfaces of the barrels and action with lamp black enables the gunmaker to achieve proper metal-to-metal tolerances.

to an angle which will ensure proper bolting and bore registration from breech to muzzle. Once this has been achieved, the lumped barrels are carefully aligned, joined, tacked, and clamped.

Next, the top and bottom ribs are carefully filed to fit flush to the barrel contours. The fore-end loop ("hanger") is also fitted at this time. Barrel ribs can be joined with lead, tin, or brazing. As a compromise, many gunmakers prefer tin. However, not just any tin will suffice. It must be pure tin. In order to test for purity, the gunmaker does what is known in the trade as making the tin "cry." By simply wobbling a shiny tin strip back and forth and listening to it creak or "cry," the trained gunmaker can determine its purity. Just another example of how men and materials work together in ways a machine alone could never duplicate.

Prior to soldering the ribs on with tin, archlike supports are fashioned from nails, then placed along the ribs and bound onto the barrels with tie wire at various intervals. In the gun trade, this process is referred to as "nailing the ribs." Proper positioning of the ribs is attained by twisting, then tightening, the tie wire around the nails at appropriate locations along the barrels. Once the gunmaker is satisfied with the results, the ribs are soldered in place with tin, using a noncorrosive flux to prevent rusting between ribs and barrels. After the ribs have been soldered, the gunmaker tests the soundness of the assembly by "ringing the barrels." Held in suspension by a wire around the forward lump, the barrel assembly is gently tapped along the barrels and ribs with a small hammer. If there are no air pockets between the soldered ribs, the barrels will ring like fine chimes.

For those squint-eyed shooters whose vision lingers on the rib and bead before firing, gunmakers have developed a nice variety of top ribs to satisfy their customers. From ventilated to swamped and from file-cut flat to elevated, ribs are designed to direct the shooter's sight from the barrels to the target. Classic game guns are most often fitted with some version of the swamped rib. This rib conforms to the contour of the barrels, usually ending just below the top of the barrels at the muzzle. The top surface of this rib is slightly concave and is finished smooth, save for the gunmaker's name and address. If the barrel set is one of two, three, etc., the barrel set number is inlaid in gold on the top rib near the breech end of the barrels, perhaps surrounded by a modest flourish of scroll engraving.

Some shooters prefer a file-cut rib or ventilated rib which they feel reduces glare and dissipates barrel heat more readily. While these ribs may give some advantage to the "groove" shooter of trap and skeet, they are of little value to the hunter who instinctively focuses his eyes on the game bird, not the gunbarrels.

Final barrel reaming on an English "best" game gun is accomplished entirely by hand. The chamber is cut from the breech end with a chamber reamer, and the choke, cut from the breech end as well, is made with a choke reamer. Chamber and head-space reaming must be done with considerable care to ensure correct support of the cartridge head. Even a fractional deviation in head spacing can cause a gun to recoil harshly as the cartridges slam back against the standing breech; under-reaming will prevent the barrels from closing at the breech.

When the desired dimensions are achieved, the internal surfaces of the barrels are hand-lapped to a mirror-like finish. Lapping is an ancient procedure (some primitive peoples used a form of it to polish the interiors of their blow guns). By passing a hard wood or soft metal plug through the bore, along with an abrasive powder and oil, the tradesman polishes the bores and closes the metal pores. It is a time-consuming process that must be guided by knowledgeable hands to assure proper finishing.

After lapping, the barrel set is subjected to machining so that the chopper lumps and barrel flats can be shaped and prepared for jointing into the action by the action filer. The fore-end loop (hanger) and extractor channel are machined at this time as well. During every phase of the barrelmaking process, the tubes are inspected for uniformity, concentricity, contour, and straightness.

Using the "thickness of smoke" from his lampblack lamp to attain precise tolerances, the action filer fits the extractor and joints the barrels to the action. Over the years, master gunbuilders have developed various procedures for handling gun parts. The barrels, for instance, are always held muzzle down between the knees during the assembly of a double gun. This gives the gunmaker two free hands in which to operate the opening lever and guide the tight-fitting barrel lumps into the action. Such a procedure guards against marring the bearing surfaces and keeps scratches ("grinners") to a minimum. The front lug of the double underlugged barrel is filed to bear perfectly on the hinge pin of the action.

For safety's sake and proper functioning of the gun, it is imperative that the breech end of the barrels form a strong gas seal at the standing breech. Again, lampblack is continually applied to all bearing surfaces until a uniform thickness-of-smoke tolerance is achieved throughout by the action filer. An almost imperceptible space is built in between the barrel flats and water table for stress purposes. Were the barrels fitted to bear snugly on all surfaces, the dynamic forces unleashed during firing would soon loosen the joint or, worse yet, crack the frame. The barreled action is then sent in the white to a proofing house in Birmingham or London where it is nitro-proofed with heavy test loads. Should the barrels or the action fail to withstand the pressures generated by the proof loads, they are discarded for scrap and the entire barrelmaking procedure is repeated.

Sideplate and fore-end iron (top and bottom) prior to hand-filing and burnishing.

PROOFING

Proofing in England was established early in the seventeenth century. Colonial expansion had created quite a brisk trade in firearms, and more than a few unscrupulous makers capitalized on it by selling shotguns and rifles that did strange things when the triggers were pulled. To ensure a high standard of quality, the London Gunmaker's Company was founded in 1637 as a proof house for England's gunmakers. The official Birmingham Proof House was established almost 200 years later by an act of Parliament. Before this 1813 act was implemented, a number of private proof houses were operated by the trade in Birmingham, notably the gunmakers Galton and Ketland. Interestingly enough, Ketland's private proof marks were eventually adopted as the official proof marks by the Birmingham Proof House.

Additional proof acts were passed by Parliament in 1868, 1950, and 1954. The high standard of quality set down by these acts has elevated the prestige of London- and Birmingham-proofed guns worldwide. Before being sold, new and altered used guns, by law, are subject to proofing in England. New guns are given two sets of proof marks. The first, or Provisional Proof, is applied to the unfinished barrel assembly, while the Definitive Proof is stamped on barrel actions tested and inspected either in the white or finished. Any used gun whose proof is questionable or has been altered by sleeving, boring, choking, etc., must be resubmitted for nitro-proofing and appropriately stamped.

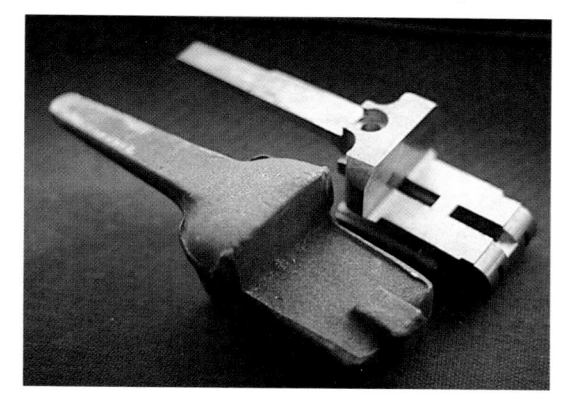

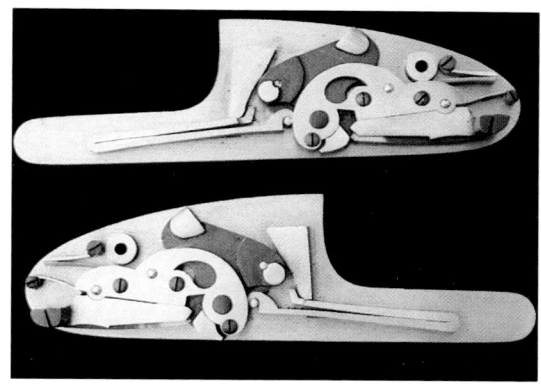

Drop-forged action body (top) is machined and hand-filed to fit desired gauge and weight of gun. Locks (bottom) are filed and fitted with the precision of a Swiss movement.

Because the British, by and large, build their game guns to accommodate a specific shotshell size and load, they are very particular about proofing. American manufacturers, on the other hand, compensate for the lack of an official proof house (that's right—there is no official U.S. proof house) by constructing thick-barreled, heavy-framed shotguns regardless of gauge or loading. But, a few American gunmakers are finally beginning to see the light and are building smoothbores trimmed in weight and profile.

Proofing of sporting arms varies considerably from country to country. The English prefer to proof and pattern each gun with a load half again as potent as it was designed to shoot. In Spain, every double gun receives a heavy proof load regardless of preferred loading.

There are numerous articles that thoroughly describe the various proofing techniques, proof marks, and proof houses which have evolved over the years. No technique, however, can duplicate the precision and style developed by a certain English octogenarian. To test the smoothbores built and repaired in his shop, this crafty old gunmaker simply aimed his shotguns out the window at the large chimney of a popular pub across the street and discharged them. By watching the brick and mortar dust fly, he could determine pattern density without a whole lot of fuss. Unfortunately, before he could patent his half-a-century-old procedure, he aimed a waterfowl gun at the chimney. When its twin three-inch magnum 12-gauge loads doubled upon firing, the beleaguered old chimney toppled, crushing twenty cars parked on the street below. The local constabulary, normally immune to gunmakers' idiosyncrasies, converged on the shop with a fistful of fines that permanently cramped the old gunnie's style.

In England, proofing involves much more than testing a barreled action's ability to withstand a stiff load. Head spacing, barrel flats, water table tolerances, bolting dynamics, barrel wall thickness and concentricity, choking, and other factors are checked before a "best" gun receives the proof house's stamp of approval. A double gun inspected and passed by either the Birmingham or London proof house carries the highest standards in the firearms industry.

Once proofed, the barrels are ready for final choking, a procedure which has been veiled in secrecy by gunmakers for generations. There are four basic methods used to choke shotgun barrels, none of which are very mysterious at all. They include swage, traditional, recessed, and reverse choking. Mass producers of single-barrel

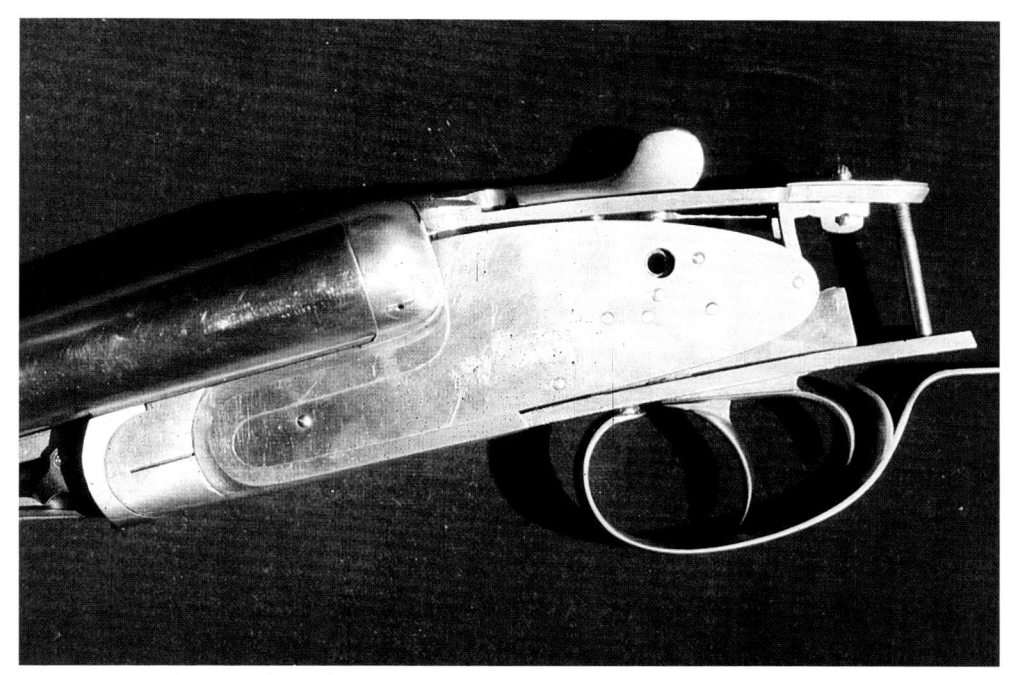

Beginning with crude drop forgings, the action filer and lockmaker render formless metal into a functional, "in the white" unit.

shotguns use the swage method (a small constriction made ½- to ¾-inch from the muzzle) because of its ease of manufacture. For those requiring rapid shot dispersal for close-range shooting of birds or targets, the reverse choke is used.

The traditional method of choking, however, still reigns supreme in England because it can be reamed and adjusted with a minimum of effort. There are some master gunbuilders who, through many years of trial and error, have developed an almost sixth sense about what must be done during traditional choking to coax the best patterns from a given load and set of barrels. In this instance, a machine is truly no match for the skilled hands of a master craftsman.

Standard choke constrictions in England are classified as follows: cylinder, quarter choke (improved-cylinder), half choke (modified), three-quarter choke (improved-modified), and full choke. Choking can also be referred to as points of constriction with full choke showing forty points of constriction, three-quarter choke equaling thirty points, and so on until true cylinder (no choke) is reached. Regardless of choke degree, maximum results are realized when the most critical element of this choking process is achieved—the proper forcing cone angle (at both the chamber and the choke) for the desired load.

English "best" gunmakers take considerable time to adjust choke so that they will maximize the effectiveness of the particular load the gun has been built to shoot. Unlike most repeaters, the English game gun is a specific tool required to perform a specific task. As such, a gun made to efficiently handle $3\frac{1}{4}$ dram equivalent, one-ounce loads of No. $7\frac{1}{2}$ shot, will be hard pressed to capably digest $3\frac{3}{4}$ dram equivalent, $1\frac{3}{4}$-ounce loads of No. 4 shot. Because their game guns are custom tailored for specific loads, the British can make and sell more shotguns and extra barrel sets, a marketing concept that has been replaced in America with interchangeable choke tubes.

Once the chokes have been adjusted to throw the proper percentage of shot in a thirty-inch circle at twenty-five to forty yards, the barrels are prepared for final finishing. Already mirror bright inside and out, the barrels' exterior is completely burnished by hand. Using a smooth steel file, the craftsman closes the steel pores on the barrels, thus burnishing them to a glasslike finish. Burnishing ensures that cold rust-bluing, the final step in the barrelmaking process, is accomplished with optimum results. After burnishing, and just prior to the cold rust-bluing procedure, the barrels are sent to the engraving shop where the gunmaker's name and address are inscribed, along with any additional embellishment.

Prior to bluing, the barrel assembly is boiled to remove grease and other surface contaminants, then the breech and muzzles are pegged (to facilitate handling during the rust-bluing process) and plugged (to prevent the solution from rusting the bores). A chemical bath is prepared, the ingredients of which vary from maker to maker and remain guarded trade secrets, and the barrels are completely submerged in the solution. The chemicals superficially rust the metal and react with it in a way that creates a final finish which ranges from pale blue to almost black in appearance. Each day, during the two- to three-week process, the barrels are removed from the solution, allowed to dry, then sanded ("carded") with progressively finer grades of steel brushes and sandpaper to remove the light layer of rust. The blue-black finish which is eventually achieved actually becomes part of the steel, not just a superficial coating. Properly cared for, cold rust-bluing on an English "best" gun will endure for generations.

Occasionally one will see the barrel-blacking process carried one step further. Tradition has dictated that proper English game-gun receivers be casehardened. However, in the case of "funeral" or "black widow" guns, receivers, sideplates, and fore-end furniture are given the same blacking that is applied to the barrels. Whether such guns were initially conceived and produced to honor royal widows at funeral ceremonies is unknown. The blackened guns are often boldly

A wide assortment of hand files and chisels are essential tools of the trade for the veteran action filer.

contrasted with gold inlay work, resembling in many respects Winchester's Model 21 Grand American. On the whole, such guns are extremely rare and were produced more to satisfy a customer's request than to display the gunmaker's consummate talents. The guns are intriguing and, despite their somber facade, are still as lethal on game as traditionally adorned sidelocks.

Barrel length on game guns has remained a moot point ever since Mr. Churchill introduced his radical twenty-five-inch concept back in the 1920s. Their debut came at a time when the shooting fraternity in England and elsewhere was still courting the long, graceful tubes left over from the black-powder and Damascus-barrel era. Churchill created quite a stir among gun writers of the day with his stubby, twenty-five-inch barrels, and to help cushion some of the shock he even designed a specially tapered rib that gave an optical illusion of length to the barrels. Today, even after the sad demise of the Churchill company, gunmakers in Europe and the U.S. are keeping the twenty-five-inch concept alive for those instinctive shooters who pursue such game birds as grouse and woodcock that demand quick gun-handling in thick cover.

While some upland hunters champion these short barrels, other traditionalists cling to 28-, 29-, or 30-inch tubes. It is truly amazing that so much controversy can be generated over that 2-inch or 3-inch difference in barrel length. Barrel length, then, remains an individual preference where there is really no right or wrong (when kept between twenty-five and thirty inches), but such spirited debate among serious shooters helps keep things interesting. After all, anyone caught hunting upland birds with a game gun whose barrels are any longer or shorter than $27\frac{1}{2}$ inches should hang up his game bag—see what I mean?

Barrelmaking the traditional way is a very painstaking and time-consuming process. It is little wonder that the price quoted for a best-quality game gun quickly reaches the five-figure mark.

THE ACTION BODY

While the barrels are being manufactured, another very important aspect of a game gun's construction is also taking shape—the action body. With little more than a hammer, sharp steel chisels, and files, the action filer converts a crude steel drop-forging into a receiver that gracefully accepts both engraving and barrels. The action body is the anvil on which the multiple stresses of shotgun recoil are received. The hammering it takes over the years demands that a forging of high-quality steel be used.

Always cognizant of the various stresses that come to bear on gun steel, a gunmaker selects forged material that will endure the rigors of firing. Action bodies are filed from forgings of mild casehardening steel known as N-32-B in the English gun trade. Forging causes the steel's grain structure to accept the flex and flow of recoil without fatiguing. Its metallurgical resilience is far superior to castings, and yet it is malleable enough to be worked into numerous receiver configurations.

Depending on gauge, the action filer contours each receiver to its proper scale. Both action size and gun weight are predetermined by a measurement of the distance "between centers." The gunmaker simply measures the distance between the "striker" (firing pin) holes and scales the action body accordingly. Currently, the standard centers for the various gauges are: $1\frac{1}{10}$-inch to $1\frac{1}{8}$-inch for 12-gauge, $1\frac{1}{16}$-inch for 16-gauge, 1 inch for 20-gauge, $\frac{15}{16}$-inch for 28-gauge, and $\frac{7}{8}$-inch for .410. An extremely light upland 12-gauge gun, for example, would be built with 1-inch centers, while a heavy wildfowling 12-gauge might require centers as wide as $1\frac{1}{4}$-inch. The centers also determine the thickness of the barrels for the gauge. Obviously, a 12-gauge with 1-inch centers would require considerably thinner tubes than one built around $1\frac{1}{4}$-inch centers. Profile templates are also used to scale and proportion in the action body.

Over the years, England's gun trade settled on two unique types of sidelock mechanisms—the bar-action and the back-action. Both deliver exceptional trigger-pulls, and when properly constructed are long lived. The bar-action gets its name from the metal inletting which takes place along the bar of the action (side of the receiver) to house the sidelock mainspring. Some contend that such inletting weakens the bar of the action and thus prefer the back-action sidelock, especially in lightweight guns of Lancaster's 12/20 persuasion.

Many of the same methods used to construct fine game guns can be applied to sporting arms of any configuration, here a double rifle.

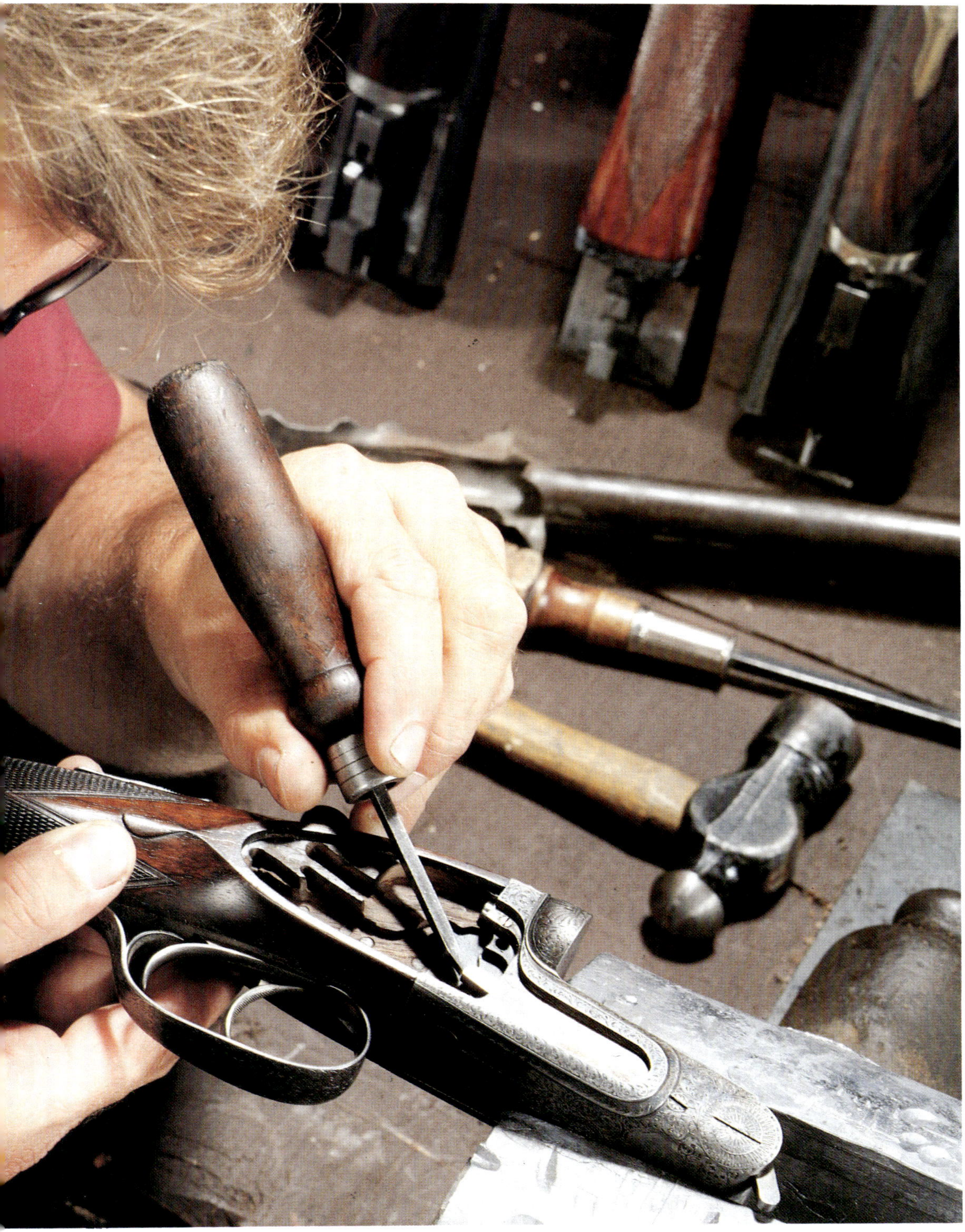

Far less metal is removed from the bar of the action to inlet a back-action sideplate. But, as with most things, you don't get something for nothing, and somewhat more inletting is required in the jaws of the stock to accommodate the back-action mainspring. The strength advantage of the back-action versus the bar-action may have had some validity in the old days, but today's modern alloy steels make the selection of either action type more personal preference than anything else.

A quick inspection of a sidelock's external pin arrangement will identify the bar-action from the back-action. If a pin exists in the sideplate's narrow leading portion that inlets into the action bar, it is a bar-action sidelock. The pin attaches the long bar-action mainspring to the sideplate. The back-action, of course, has no pin in this area of the sideplate. Boss and Stephen Grant game guns are classic examples of the back-action sidelock.

Hammer and chisels are used to rough out the action, cut all the beads around the fences, and prepare the frame for the lock mechanism. It is tedious, grueling work. The action filer develops forearm and shoulder muscles as rigid as the steel he sculpts. This is especially true if he is working on rough forgings that have had little or no machining done to them. Clamped firmly in the lead-shrouded jaws of a vise, the forged action is first chiseled to the appropriate shape with the help of a sizing template and jig. All the while, the action filer must work to ensure a proper angle at the standing breech and water table (action flats) for barrelfitting and jointing. This roughing-out procedure often requires two to three weeks of daily labor.

Each steel forging, even from identical lots of steel, has its own unique grain structure which must be compensated for by the action filer throughout building of the action. He must file with the flow of the grain. Once the action shape has been reduced to the prescribed conformation, it is hand-filed to remove chisel marks and "grinners." Thickness of smoke is the inescapable law of the traditional English gun trade, and lampblack is used by the action filer to smoke the forward chopper lump ("hook") and joint the barrels onto the hinge pin of the receiver to the proper tolerances. Wherever the bearing surfaces scrape away the black smoke, the action filer gradually reduces these high spots until a perfect meeting of metal to metal is achieved. Such fine tolerances could be achieved by sophisticated tape milling machines, but due to the idiosyncrasies of the various gun steels, the machine cuts could also conflict with the grain pattern of the metal and create uneven wear. Built with skilled hands, a best-quality game gun wears together, not apart.

To prepare the surface of the action body for engraving and casehardening, the action filer closes the grain of the metal with burnishing strokes, then finishes the action to a chrome-like luster with fine emery cloth.

With this accomplished, the next step involves hand-filing the receiver hardware—the trigger guard, bow, triggers, top lever, safety catch, cocking rods, and fore-end furniture. Historically, the English gun trade fashioned all of these items from drop-forgings (often referred to as "stampings"). However, because of the serious attrition in the ranks of master gunbuilders and their attendant suppliers, a few parts, such as the safety catch and top lever, are often made from rough castings. Although a departure from tradition, the parts are still carefully fitted and finished by hand. But there are those who consider such castings a travesty to the trade.

To gain entrance into England's prestigious Worshipful Master Gunbuilder's Guild, a gunmaker must be capable of building a best-quality game gun from a chunk of walnut and a billet of steel, using only hand tools. For obvious reasons, only a handful of craftsmen are proficient enough to complete such a demanding task. This is precisely why the cost of building a fine game gun by hand is so high and the wait so long. Quality cannot be rushed, and neither can the tradesman who invests a great deal of pride in every task he performs.

In America's and Europe's headlong rush to answer every firearm production challenge with the unfeeling efficiency of a machine, it is comforting to know there are still those who are strangers to the assembly line. In English gunbuilding circles, craftsmanship is almost a trade unto itself. And while many game gun artisans in England remain chattel in the hands of the company's board of directors, they are, to a man, fiercely proud of their work. It is little wonder the trade attracts and breeds individuals of such rare talent and character. With chisel or file, a "gunnie's" loyalty belongs strictly to the task at hand—royalty, gentry, and politics notwithstanding.

The action filer's task is multifaceted. His intimacy with the internal and external mechanics of gunbuilding must be profound. Fashioned by hand, the trigger-guard bow and strap are actually two pieces of forged steel that are welded together by the action filer. The forward end of the bow has a quarter-inch appendage which is threaded and screwed flush into the underside of the receiver just ahead of the front trigger.

The triggers, also hand-filed from stampings, are canted to the left or right depending on the handedness of the shooter. Such an arrangement enables a shooter to shift comfortably and quickly from one trigger to the next. On best-quality guns, the front trigger is often hinged ("articulated") to prevent any bruising of the trigger finger from recoil when the rear trigger is pulled. This seldom occurs with light game loads, but the hinged trigger can be a convenience when the gun is improperly gripped during a hastily mounted shot. Triggers on most game guns are adjusted to release crisply, the front at $3\frac{1}{2}$ pounds and the rear at 4.

Like all fine mechanisms brought to the pinnacle of development, the British sidelock shotgun created a plethora of ingenious patents and refinements. After automatic ejectors reached near perfection, top name gunmakers jockeyed for prominence by introducing various self-opening and assisted-opening sidelock guns. Such guns were touted for their ease of loading, especially during the rapid-fire action encountered during driven-bird shoots. This option, considered by some American gun writers as frivolous, was quickly accepted by the shooting fraternity in England, where etiquette dictates that gentlemen *do not* load their own guns.

The difference between an assisted-opening gun and a true self-opener becomes immediately apparent when the top lever is activated. A true self-opener will break open the action and eject spent cartridges without help from the shooter. The assisted-opener, on the other hand, partially lifts the barrels from the action but

A best-quality sidelock double rifle receives final adjustment.

requires an additional assist from the shooter to complete the opening and ejecting process. Both designs are frequently found on best-quality sidelocks.

However, these designs are not without their drawbacks. Those who enjoy such ease in opening also strengthen their forearms when they close these guns. In America, where loader and shooter are one and the same, self- and assisted-opening guns do not have the same appeal as they do among the shooting gentry of England who use loaders to feed cartridges into their matched pairs behind the butts.

Apparently, Westley Richards of England has been the only gunmaker to successfully construct a self-opening boxlock gun. Why the guns were never produced in any great number is still unknown. Whatever one's preference, the assisted- and self-opening designs are proof again of England's centuries-long quest to perfect the sidelock game gun. Few other gunmaking countries can claim such a commitment to innovation and excellence.

Though refined into reliable mechanisms over the years, single triggers have little place on true classic game guns. Despite all the howls of protest to the contrary, double triggers afford a smoother and more immediate selection of barrels no single-selective trigger can duplicate. Whether a far-flushing pheasant or a high-flying driven partridge, the desired barrel and choke combination can be quickly selected on a double-trigger game gun. With a little practice, any shooter possessing average dexterity can master the use of double triggers. The likelihood of malfunction is also minimized by double triggers, with each trigger activating its own lock. Most single-trigger mechanisms rely on recoil and there's an additional, though subconscious, trigger-pull to contend with to fire the second barrel.

In all fairness, the modern single-selective trigger is of little hindrance to the waterfowler, as he usually has ample time to choose chokings. In this regard, of all of the double guns built to endure the rigors of heavy loads and cruel weather, Winchester's Model 21 has few equals. It also possesses one of the best single-selective triggers ever designed. Though never a truly hand-built double, its simple bolting system and superior steels enable it to digest caseloads of shells without a quiver. (The aforementioned plaudits should prove that the author is not a total Anglophile in his taste for quality smoothbores.)

The action filer's next task is to shape and assemble the fore-end iron. At first glance, the scanty fore-end on a game gun appears to be somewhat of an afterthought. In addition to completing the gun's assembly, the fore-end houses the ejector mechanisms which extract and eject cartridges from the barrels. Most game gun fore-ends are fitted with the very simple Anson pushrod fastener device and a compact Southgate ejector system. Both designs have changed little since their inception almost a century ago, and have proven very reliable down through the years. When depressed, the spring-loaded pushrod disengages from the barrel hook to allow removal of the fore-end, affording quick disassembly of the shotgun.

Working in tandem, each Southgate ejector mechanism consists of only two components, a spring and a tumbler commonly referred to as a "kicker." Upon firing, a cam rod is activated in the action body, and the kicker is tripped by the ejector spring when the barrels are pivoted open. Whether sidelock or boxlock, most ejectors are cocked in basically the same fashion. Properly regulated and timed, the ejectors will place ejected shells within a few inches of each other on the ground.

Every part in the fore-end assembly is carefully hand-filed to fit and then burnished to assure smooth operation. During production, the ejector mechanisms are left in the white while the pushrod and fore-end housing are prepared for casehardening or bluing.

That portion of the fore-end that rotates upon the action-body knuckle when the gun is opened and closed is smoked with lampblack and filed until it bears evenly; sloppy metalwork here would cause ejection and lock-up problems down the road. On many European doubles, the tapered portions of the fore-end iron that extend over the top of the action body are filed to meet flush with the receiver. This is done more for eye relief than anything else, and over years of service may eventually loosen the fore-end assembly. Many English double-gun makers leave a very slight gap at this juncture to enable the fore-end iron and receiver to wear together, not apart.

Contrary to popular belief, a shotgun's action that is hard to open and close does not mean that the gun has good tolerances. What it does indicate is a lack of time and care spent by the gunmaker to properly adjust the final fit. The tightness results from too much steel left on the parts to compensate for hasty production.

LOCKMAKING

The sidelock shotgun has remained a classic, not so much because its locks are marginally safer than other designs, but because it satisfies both esthetic form and function. Its graceful lines please the discriminating shooter's pride of ownership, while its reliable lockwork delivers crisp trigger-pulls even after caseloads of cartridges have passed through the barrels. When Britain ruled the waves, it was imperative that the sporting arms carried to the far corners of the earth be fitted with actions as durable and tough as the Isles' conquering spirit.

Whether removed by a hand-detachable transverse pin or by a screwdriver, the lock mechanisms on a sidelock gun are readily accessible. The sidelock mechanism consists of twelve basic parts, each specifically hardened and tempered to perform its special function. The two sear springs, mainspring, bridle, two sear pins, two tumblers, and five screws (pins) composing the sidelock must be precisely filed to shape, burnished, and securely anchored to the lockplate.

Obsessed with the importance of properly tempered gun steel, each part of an English sidelock mechanism is individually hardened at critical points by the craftsman. The mainspring, for example, is held with pliers and heated with a gas torch until a rosy red blush is achieved. The spring is then immersed in a whale-oil bath for quenching. After cooling in the whale oil, the part is retrieved and held once again in the torch's flame to burn off the remaining oil. Much to the chagrin of young apprentices, the burnt whale oil residue must be completely scrubbed off the lock parts, a tedious procedure which requires considerable time and elbow grease. Carefully tempered in this fashion, each lock part can perform for years without fatiguing or breaking.

Such careful attention to tempering is evidence again of an English gunmaker's concern for building sporting shotguns that endure the test of time. Perhaps carrying hardening to the extreme, the hammers ("tumblers") are carefully tempered in three critical areas to assure proper functioning and wear resistance. When assembled, the internal lockwork of a best-quality gun resembles the mechanism of a fine Swiss watch and will perform with the same jeweled precision.

Whether bar-action or back-action, sidelock mechanisms fitted with simple intercepting sears have been praised for their inherent safety. Should the sidelock gun be dropped or sharply jolted, the built-in safety sears intercept the hammers before they can strike the firing pins. Some boxlock guns also have intercepting sears. This advantage could prove a godsend to upland hunters who hunt in rugged terrain. Sooner or later, even the most agile of hunters will take a spill afield. The added measure of safety built into a sidelock game gun can have a definite calming effect as the years steal away a hunter's surefootedness.

Bordering on alchemy, the gunmaker's choice of shooting steel has often been shrouded in half-truths and controversy. Springmaking for locks and other mechanisms has its own aura of mystery. According to some master gunbuilders, the best raw material for springmaking was provided by the blacksmithing trade in the form of worn out horseshoes. The incessant pounding over cobblestone apparently work-hardened and tempered the shoe steel, giving it greater elasticity and durability. As farfetched as this may sound to those weaned on the scientific method, unless these empirical thinkers have ever plied a hand file to such steel and witnessed its long-term performance, their criticism should be reserved for the halls of academia.

Buried in bone charcoal (top), the action body and case-hardening box are placed in pre-heated furnace (bottom).

Many are those who profess to be expert in English, American, or European shotgun making. Generations of gunmakers have generated countless techniques and methods for building guns that continue to evolve to this day. More firearms authorities have died than will ever live again, and today, no one man could ever hope to amass the vast technical knowledge and practical experience it has taken the gun trade hundreds of years to accumulate. There are no gun experts, there are only those who realize their limitations and are humble enough to admit that they will spend a lifetime learning about guns and gunmaking.

Today, as in the past, most of the lockwork used by London and Birmingham gunmakers is jobbed out, even though a few of the best-known houses are bringing along apprentices in this demanding occupation. The contract or piece-work arrangement is characteristic of many firearms manufacturing centers around the world.

A great deal of the romance and appeal of the English "best" gun would be diminished should the buyer experience firsthand the grueling routine required to produce such a piece. Paradoxically, it is not uncommon in the trade to find craftsmen who have never hunted a day in their lives or, for that matter, even fired, save for proofing or patterning, the very guns that provide them with a livelihood. Their hours at the

A few hours later the box is removed and allowed to cool (top) before entire contents of the box are quickly cast into the quenching reservoir (bottom).

bench are usually long, their pay often paltry, and their access to gaming fields normally non-existent.

The gun trade has declined and is faltering in England today partially because the craftsmen have always been the last to share in the perks and profits of the firm. This, coupled with the sad fact that more attention was paid to courting royal tastes rather than recognizing the purchasing power of the man on the street, has left much of the trade with an onerous blue-blood reputation to uphold in a very red-blooded marketplace. Granted, regal ways have often enchanted the masses, but seldom have they paid the gunmaker's rent.

Despite ever-present poverty, it is still a wealthy world in which most Americans and Europeans live, royalty notwithstanding. With proper marketing campaigns and image building, the English-quality game gun can once again regain its rightful place in the hands of hunters and shooters worldwide. As proof that the U.S. market is being discovered and courted, officers of James Purdey & Sons make an annual selling trip to this country, taking orders, discussing guns, and expanding their knowledge of American tastes.

Once a thriving occupation, there is really only a handful of truly skilled lockmakers left in England today. A close examination of their craftsmanship makes it easy to understand why. The precision fit and finish of every part almost defies one to believe that they were fashioned by hand with simple, if not archaic, tools. Such workmanship is all the more remarkable when one realizes that function enshrouds this intricate lockwork within the inletted confines of the stock. It is difficult to appreciate the crispness of trigger-pull and the quick response of hammer to firing pin from a mechanism that seldom sees the light of day. There are even some sidelock admirers who purchase game guns with gold plated, hand-detachable locks that not only afford ease of maintenance and repair, but also allow an easy peek at the all-important lockwork.

Whether equipped with customary cocking indicators and protruding pins or without any external manifestations (as has become the fashion in Italy, though copied from the English), locks are the lifeblood of every game gun and should be selected with care.

CASEHARDENING

There are few secrets more guarded around the gun trade than the procedures and ingredients used in the color-casehardening process. There are still those old masters who would rather take their knowledge to the grave than share it with anyone, friend or foe. Part of this mystique may have evolved around the turn of the century

Little more than a thin skin of carbonized steel, casehardening strengthens the action's surface while enabling its internal metal to flex when the gun is discharged. Action, lockplate, and fore-end furniture take on case colors that range from straw and henna to cobalt blue.

when it was rumored that certain prestigious gun houses in England were using a particular "ingredient" in their charcoal to produce more vibrant case colors. Whether human bone was actually used remains a moot point, but to this day English casehardening evokes images of occult-like rituals, gurgling caldrons, and cryptic formulas applied to gun steel behind barred doors.

The purpose of casehardening is to temper and harden receivers and lockplates so they can endure the rigors of shooting. The entire casehardening process involves only three simple ingredients: bone charcoal, heat, and water. However, it is the degree to which they are applied that produces the temper and coloring most desired by the gunmaker. Furnace procedure varies in both temperature and duration, giving the gunmaker a wide range of control. The bone charcoal is usually graded fine and coarse and is made from animal bone. Considering the care taken throughout the casehardening procedure, one would think the water used in such a critical process would be distilled and maintained at some optimum temperature. More often than not, a garden hose from the tap is all that is used to fill the back-alley-variety trash can set up as a quenching reservoir.

Each gunmaker has his own pet casehardening recipe, but the procedure is essentially the same for all. Still in the white and engraved to the customer's specifications, the action body and lockplates are completely degreased with naphtha or a similar solvent just prior to casehardening. Some English gunmakers prefer to leave the lockplates and action body unassembled before they are packed in charcoal in the heavy-gauge steel box that will be placed in the furnace. While this procedure is widely used, it often leaves a thin line, almost devoid of color, around the leading edges of the lockplates and many of the screw and pin holes. In order to ensure continuity of case colors throughout lockplates and action body, many gunmakers prefer to assemble these parts before they are packed in the bone charcoal.

"Blocking" is another simple technique used to distribute case colors evenly, especially on areas of the frame where the metal is less dense, such as the back strap, receiver floor, and fore-end furniture. Heavy steel washers and bolts are wired or clamped to these areas to add mass and attract case color. Blocking is also used on the lockplates to concentrate color highlights around gold inlays and game-scene engraved areas.

The charcoal-packing process also varies throughout the trade. While some makers prefer to pack their parts in fine charcoal and cover with the coarse, others use only the heavier ground charcoal as well as chunks of leather for packing. Once the components have been packed in the bone black charcoal, a forked steel rod is used to place the charcoal box into the preheated furnace. Hardening temperatures range from 750 degrees Fahrenheit to 1500 degrees Fahrenheit with furnace time varying correspondingly from three hours to an hour and a half; the higher the temperature, the shorter duration and vice versa. Care must be taken to prevent the metal from being over-hardened, causing it to lose temper and become brittle. Proper casehardening produces only a thin carbon layer of hardness, leaving the flex characteristics of the internal metal intact; over-hardened metal often takes on a telltale carrotlike coloration.

After the crucible is removed from the furnace, it is allowed to air-cool for a short period before its contents are quenched. Again, it is the experienced eye of the craftsman that determines the correct rosy glow of the packing box prior to the casehardened part's violent emersion into the water-filled trash can.

To prevent the outside air from contracting and scaling the engraved metal gun parts, the box's contents must be swiftly and deftly plunged into the quenching can. Submerged in the quenching can is an opened mesh rack that catches the gun parts, allowing the charcoal debris to pass on through to the bottom. The parts are retrieved and then placed back into the still-hot packing box for drying.

If properly casehardened, the colors on the lockplates, action body, and fore-end furniture should range from cobalt to light blue to henna shades and straw. Depending on the steel, slight warping of the metal may occur and require springing and refitting. Some gunmakers also spray the exterior surface of casehardened parts with an industrial grade lacquer to seal in the colors. Because gun steel, even from the same batch, has unique, individual characteristics, the degree of control exercised by the gunmaker over the casehardening process is limited. Sometimes the colors dazzle, other times they disappoint; it is always a gamble.

Certain European gunmakers continue to use cyanide in their casehardening process. While some interesting colors can be obtained with this method (more than a few tiger-striped receivers are making the rounds these days), its ability to properly temper the steel is suspect. It is not a new process and was used by more than a few of America's renowned classic gunmakers before they succumbed to mass production.

While admittedly a much faster technique than the English bone-charcoal method, cyanide hardening has a number of drawbacks that should be considered. Gun parts are given a 900-degree bath of cyanide and assorted salts for three hours or longer. The relatively cold gun steel hitting the hot bath apparently creates some kind of a molecular disturbance in the metal, as cyanide-hardened steel has a much greater tendency to warp than does charcoal-hardened metal. As a result, the process often requires considerable springing and refitting of parts. Also, metal hardened in this fashion does not take on the rich color or resilient temper of gun steel treated to the slower charcoal-hardening procedure. For this reason, many European shotgun receivers are coin-finished or polished to a satin gunmetal gray.

Many of these contemporary game guns, though they may externally reflect all the beauty of the gunmaker's art, also have the reputation of giving up the ghost over the long haul. It must be remembered that the typical English gunner of yesteryear shot thousands of rounds each season. As such, his gun had to be properly tempered and hardened if it was to endure the numerous stresses such prolonged shooting can develop. Unless a gun is used extensively on the trap or skeet range, it would seldom, if ever, receive equal punishment from the average American shooter. Fortunately, many less than "best" game guns are purchased by gun collectors who are more taken by external cosmetics than the internal temperament of gun steel. Such lovingly handled double guns will no doubt endure for generations, saved from the rigors of powder and shot by their compelling beauty.

Neither is the casehardening process exclusively limited to the gun trade. Many a farmer with blowtorch in hand has also treated his tools and implements to color casehardening, however crude by comparison. There is also an apocryphal story in the gun trade about a renowned casehardener who got in a row at one of the local pubs when his ability to caseharden was questioned by a group of inebriates. To prove his uncanny prowess with bone and furnace, the man promptly produced an action body, wrapped it in newspaper, saturated the package with his urine, and stuck it deep into the glowing coals of the pub's pot-bellied stove. After an hour or so on the coals, the action was removed and, to the astonishment of everyone there assembled, the case colors were both brilliant and beautiful. Whether or not the quality or quantity of the pub's brew had anything to do with this apparently successful casehardening case history is subject to debate in the establishment to this very day.

Given the inherent strength of today's super-alloy steels, casehardening remains an anachronism in gunmaking. Tradition, like true romance, dies hard, and the colorfully casehardened game guns of a bygone era are still the standard by which many contemporary double guns are compared. Properly done, whether using bone charcoal, cyanide, or whatever, the casehardening process remains a trade secret that symbolizes the generations of pride and quality built into each "best" gun.

ANNEALING

The opposite of casehardening, annealing is a simple process that softens gun steel so that it will be more malleable in the hands of the action filer and engraver. Whenever an old shotgun is reconditioned, the receiver and fore-end steel are often annealed for refitting and re-engraving. Gun parts requiring annealing are wrapped and sealed in stainless-steel foil, placed in a 1500-degree Fahrenheit furnace for an hour or so, and then allowed to cool down overnight in the extinguished furnace. Softened in this fashion, gun steel retains its elasticity and can be casehardened again without sacrificing its tensile strength.

Such a process affords the gunmaker considerable flexibility. For example, should portions of the receiver's engraving be scaled off during casehardening, the metal can be annealed, the engraving retouched, and the steel fired once more in the bone charcoal. Quality gun steel can be annealed numerous times before it begins to lose its structural integrity.

BOLTING

Patent offices are filled with reams of designs extolling the virtues of innovative shotgun bolting devices. Intriguing though some of them may be, the mystery of surefire bolting was solved by House of Purdey almost a century ago. Purdey's double-underlug bolting design survived the transition from black to smokeless powder, successfully preventing barrels from gaping at the breech, and action bodies from cracking where the water table meets the standing breech.

Like a 1958 Cadillac decked out in fender skirts and chrome, many shotguns have been fitted with superfluous bolting appendages more to salve the psyche of the shooter than to add strength to the gun. What cleverly shaped doll's-heads, husky cross-bolts, and shapely side-clips did add to game guns was a dimension in sales appeal that delighted the derbied accountants and directors in the front office. Such ingenious devices also tended to calm the fears of shooters who were used to seeing cheap double guns with breeches that rattled like castanets.

The whip action of shotgun barrels during discharge is a phenomenon that can never really be entirely tamed. There must be some movement in the casehardened action body, or the double gun will eventually self-destruct. Gunmakers allow for this occurrence by building in an almost imperceptible degree of play between the barrel flats and the water table of the action body. Thus fitted, the double gun can flex fractionally at the breech upon firing and help dissipate the ever-present barrel whip, a simple philosophy of "bend but don't break."

Perhaps the simplest and most effective companion to double underlug bolting is the Purdey "third grip." Located midway between the breech end of the barrels and protruding about a quarter-inch, this sturdy grip is designed to fit snugly into a slot milled in the standing breech. Upon closing, it is held fast by an overbolt that functions as an integral part of the spindle and top-lever assembly. When the gun is fired, the third grip helps reduce the vertical stress associated with barrel whip.

However, little can be done to contain the lesser horizontal barrel movement. Even though side-clips may add an attractive touch of class to side-by-side doubles, they do little to alleviate the lateral barrel-stress at the breech when the gun is fired. Prolonged lateral stress on improperly fitted double guns invariably leads to gaping at the breech and eventual head-space problems.

As proof of the strength of a properly, albeit simple, underbolted double gun, one needs only to research the endurance of Winchester's legendary Model 21. After consuming thousands of proof loads during a test, the Model 21's *single* underbolt remained unaffected and entirely functional while other guns (employing every conceivable bolting device) shot loose. Thus, with today's modern alloy steels, the Purdey double underlug design is perfectly capable of providing years of safe and dependable service to the double-gun shooter with or without the romance other bolting devices may add to the gun.

However, the English need not claim all the credit for developing effective game-gun bolting mechanisms. L. C. Smith's top-action Yankee double with its unique rotary bolt design has proven almost foolproof for more than a century, the tapered bolt compensating for wear every time the action is closed. Located on top of the standing breech, farthest from the hinge pin, the bolt is in perfect position to keep the barrels snug at the breech.

While it may be comforting to hear and feel the action slamming shut, shooters can compensate for bolting stress, and thus prolong the life of their double guns, by slowly bringing the breech up to the barrels when closing the action. There are those who even advocate holding the top lever open, releasing it only after the action is closed.

By resisting the promotional supplications of ammo manufacturers to stuff their pieces with maximum or magnum loads, double-gun shooters can bequeath their shotguns to sons and heirs in fine working order. Few hunters today realize that during America's waterfowling heyday, black-powder 10-gauge doubles were effectively bringing ducks and geese to bag with only one ounce of shot. Though the macho magnum does have its place for shooting game at extreme distances, most upland game can be taken quite capably with one-ounce, low-brass loadings. One's shooting piece, shoulder, and hearing will fare better in the long run, and the game birds will fold just as impressively.

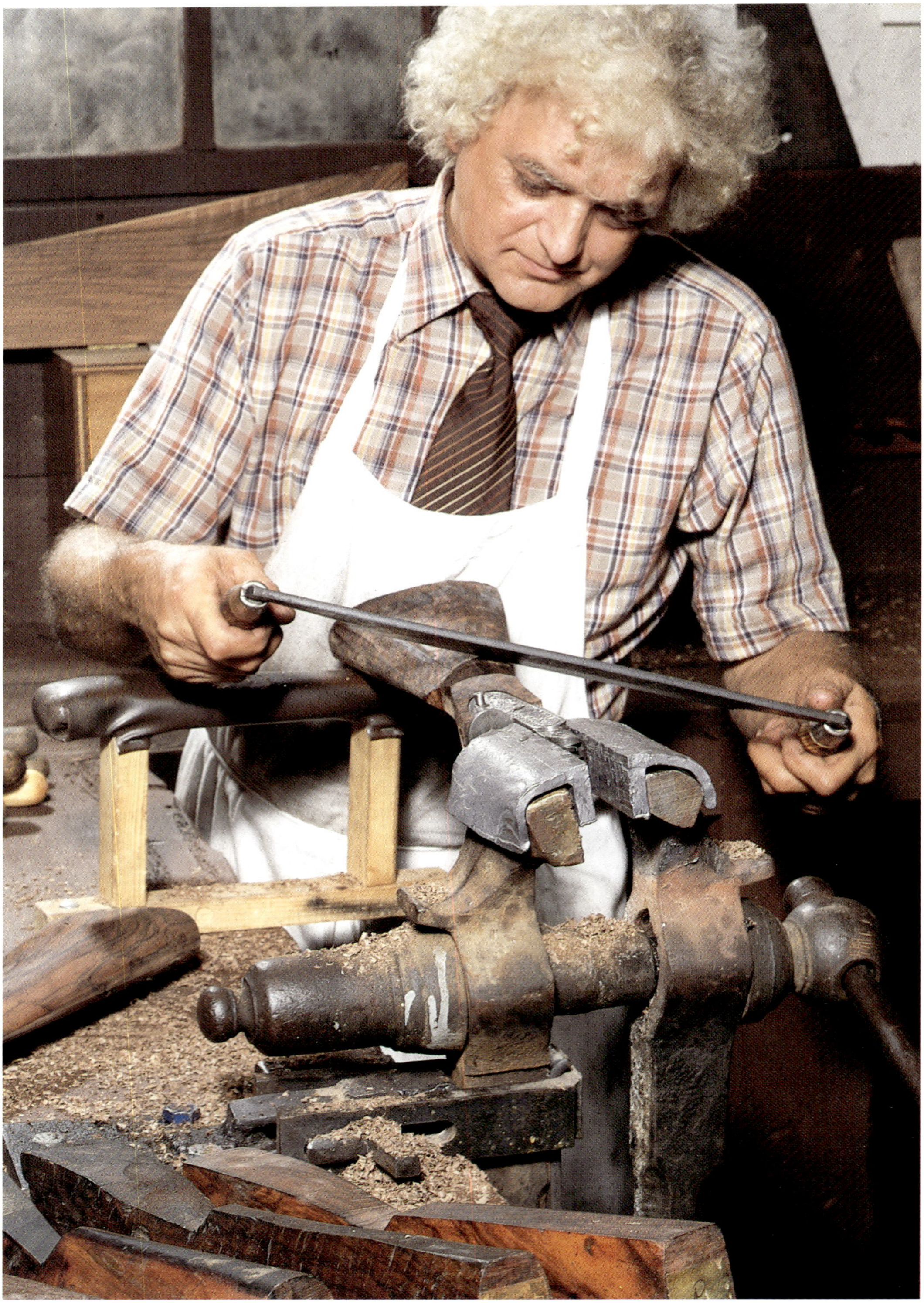

4

GOOD WOOD

GOOD WOOD, LIKE GOOD WHISKEY, mellows with age. Whether French, Circassian, English, or American, properly aged walnut has remained the stockmaker's choice for centuries. Durable, lightweight, and pleasing to the eye, the workability of walnut transcends that of all other wood types.

Over the years, walnut has been tested for its crush resistance, tensile strength, and innate stability. Its only real drawback is its increasing scarcity. The same population boom that spawned the mass-produced, repeating shotgun has also taken its toll on the world's walnut supply. World War II also devastated much of Europe's walnut forests, while cabinetmakers and other users of veneers continue to cut into America's supply of black walnut trees. As a result, it is not uncommon to hear of a walnut tree being sold for many thousands of dollars, and roots and all are harvested.

But what really constitutes good wood in the hands and minds of today's custom stockmakers? Selection of game gun wood is a science unto itself, requiring a thorough knowledge of gunmaking dynamics. The English have always had a penchant for rather dark, straight-grained French walnut, showing very little of the tiger striping or marble-cake swirls commonly found in highly figured American walnut. English stockers select blanks that exhibit layered contrasts of brown, black, and auburn grain patterns.

Always uppermost in a game gun maker's mind is that a blank's grain structure must run straight and knotless through the hand (grip) of the stock. Should uneven grain structure or wood flaws exist in the wrist section of a sidelock gun, chances are good that the stock will crack or split around the safety (top) tang and sideplates from recoil.

Just as English and European walnut are touted for denseness of grain, American black walnut is often criticized for its comparative porosity. In most cases, a woodfiller must be applied to American walnut before final finishing. American stockers will often employ a tinted woodfiller to highlight the walnut's natural liver-ticked color.

Because American walnut is porous in nature and has a tendency to warp, many gun makers, and a few custom stockers, prefer to use only European walnut. One must also remember that the building of an English game gun is strictly a labor-intensive process, and if the gunmaker can avoid the additional step of applying woodfiller to walnut, he will do so. European walnut, though sometimes not as dramatic in figure as American claro or black walnut, remains the standard wood choice of England's and Europe's premier game gun makers.

Most of the wood fitted to English game guns originates from the root portions of slow-growing French walnut trees. Even though interesting grain patterns can be found in crotch sections of the tree, the most dramatic wood figure resides in the root. Root sections tend to be denser in grain structure, which makes for a sturdier stock and one that will also take and hold checkering and carving more readily. Pipemakers will often use discarded portions of burl walnut to construct some rather elegant-looking smoking vessels.

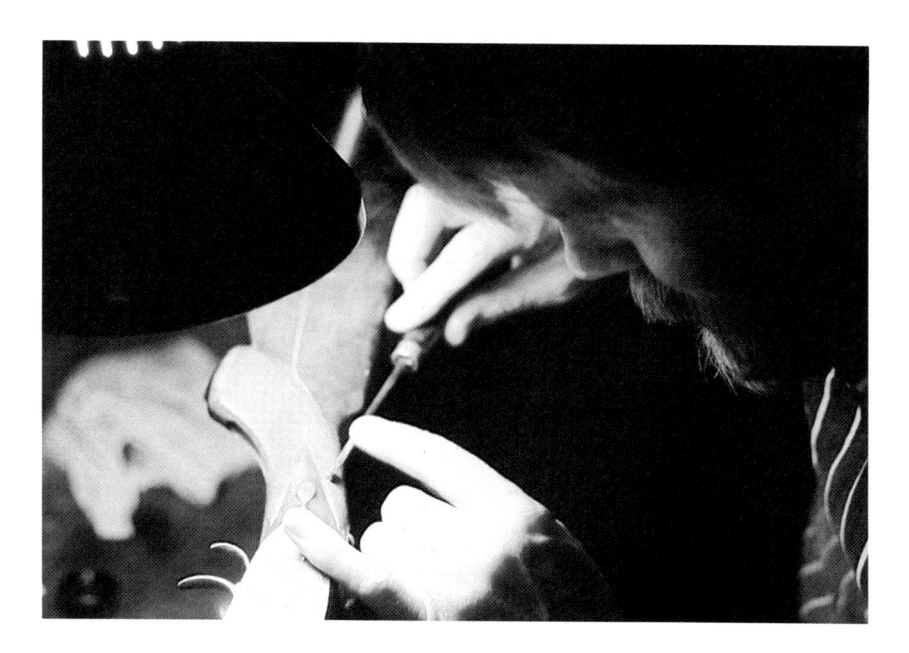

But as beautiful as burl walnut can be, it is also brittle, often exhibiting a capricious grain structure that can cause problems during shaping and finishing. Burl can be exhilarating to behold near the stock's butt, but should never be found in the hand area of the gun. The stockmaker's ultimate goal, of course, is to blend both beauty and utility in such a way that the finished product complements the shooter's ability, while complimenting the gunmaker's as well.

Once a prudent job of cutting is made by the supplier to provide wood with the most attractive figure, the stockmaker's first task is to envision how the rough blank should best be inletted to accept the action. This requires a great degree of knowledge about walnut behavior and the stress imparted by gun steel during recoil. To maintain continuity of grain pattern and wood color, both the buttstock and forearm should be taken from the same blank of wood. Tapering in width from around $6\frac{1}{2}$ inches at the butt to $2\frac{1}{2}$ inches or so at the hand, each roughed-out blank is approximately three inches thick.

Using the measurements from the try-gun fitting, the stockmaker selects the appropriate template to trace the length of pull and "bend" (i.e., drop at comb and drop at heel) of the stock. The template, a quarter-inch-thick silhouette of a finished stock configuration, once traced, approximates the final shape the buttstock will take.

Using the trace dimensions as a guide, the stockmaker must next "cut the wood over" with a sharp wood chisel and draw knife. Beginning at the butt-end and working toward the hand, the stockmaker removes the surplus wood from the blank. The entire block is then warmed slightly with a flame to determine if there are any serious flaws ("shakes") in the wood.

Although seeming somewhat contrary to logic, the blank at this time is cut to length from the head-end and warmed once again. Then measuring from the butt-end of the blank, the stocker determines the required length with his length stick and adds the difference between the front trigger and the back of the action to his overall measurement. The only dimension the template cannot transfer onto the stock blank is that of cast, that slight amount of lateral offset built into the stock to facilitate proper gun mounting and sight alignment. Normally ranging from

Destined for the stockmaker's bench, walnut blanks (top) must be properly air-dried before they are wed to gun steel. Using a variety of wood chisels and gouges, the stockmaker inlets top straps and jaws of buttstock (bottom).

⅛ inch to ½ inch or more, cast-off (lateral offset to the right) accommodates righthanded shooters while cast-on (lateral offset to the left) is added for lefthanders. The stockmaker adjusts for cast by inletting the head-end of the stock into the safety tang and back of the action at the desired lateral angle, left or right. He determines this by finding the center line at the butt-end of the stock and marking the prescribed amount either to the left or right of the line, depending on

Culmination of the "stocker's labor" is a buttstock that is functionally elegant, finely checkered, and oil finished.

the cast desired. At this point, the action is clamped to the head-end of the stock with a G-clamp, and the blank and barreled action are mounted as a unit in a cast-off jig. Again, the angle at which the blank is clamped to the action will determine the amount of cast-off/cast-on desired in the gun. All that remains at this stage is for the stockmaker to carefully trace in pencil around the safety tang (action strap) to outline the inletting angle.

The drop measurements of the stock, both at the comb and at the heel, have already been traced onto the buttstock via the appropriate template. If there is such a thing as standard or average drop dimensions in game gun stocking, they would be about 2⅛ inches to 2¼ inches at the heel and around 1½ inches at the comb. The British do like their game guns straight!

In order to compensate for the prescribed drop dimensions during inletting of the strap and the back face of the action, additional drop must be allowed. For instance, if the desired drop at the heel is to be 2¼ inches, at least three inches must be figured on because as the back strap is inletted at its down-sweeping angle into the blank, the barrels will be raised approximately three-quarters of an inch.

Without the proper tools, precise inletting of the stock would be impossible. And while the stockmaker's selection of tools may vary, depending on personal preference, all would agree that high-quality wood chisels are essential. Some of the other tools used by the stocker include: a hand reamer (drill), screwdriver assortment, bradawl, surform, draw knife, a good set of files, and, occasionally, a spoke shaver.

But it is really the chisels and gouges (rounded chisels) that perform the lion's share of the tasks required of the stockmaker. Of the ten or more basic chisels used (and still being made), a few specialized chisels such as the bottoming and foot chisels must be custom-made by the stocker. Such unique tools enable the stockmaker to feel his way into the dark nooks and crannies encountered during the inletting of the action as well as tight spots around the fore-end metal.

In order to prevent the stress factors of recoil from splitting or cracking the buttstock around the back strap and lockplates, the stockmaker must achieve a uniform bearing of wood against metal at the back face of the action. When the action is let up into the head of the stock, care must also be taken to remove only that amount of wood which will enable the hammers to function properly without bearing against the wood. To offset the stress of recoil, as much wood as possible should be left undisturbed in the head or "horn" of the stock. In some areas between the locks and action, as little as $1/16$-inch of wood is all that remains after inletting—further underscoring the necessity for precise craftsmanship in the stocking of a sidelock gun.

Good Wood

Before putting chisel to wood, the stockmaker must first translate the try-gun dimensions. Length, cast, bend, etc., must be precisely calculated prior to inletting.

Stockmaking produces its fair share of the genuine characters that constitute the English gun trade. Often passionately committed to achieving excellence in their work, old-school stockers sometimes pay dearly for their dedication. One such fellow, in the process of stocking a "best" sidelock, violated one of the cardinal rules of stockmaking (that of keeping both hands on the tool), slipped with his chisel, and severely gouged his thumb. Instead of seeking medical attention, the stalwart stocker heated a tin of varnish and poured it over his spurting thumb to cauterize the wound.

Three days later, after finishing the stocking job he promised his customer, the pain in his thumb became intolerable. The doctor he consulted took one look at the badly infected thumb and, without knowing his patient's profession, said, "So, how is the gun trade these days?" Apparently the good doctor had similar encounters with other gunnies and realized that only someone in the trade would pull such an incredible stunt. The stockmaker wasn't able to save face that day, but the doctor did manage to save his thumb.

Throughout the stocking process, one critical factor remains constant: wood quality. A properly sawn and air-dried blank becomes clay in the hands of a skilled stockmaker. The English have always prided themselves on their use of ancient, air-dried blanks. However, for the sake expedience, most of the wood supplied to the trade today, whether in England, Spain, Italy, France, or the U.S., is kiln-dried. For the most part, it is no longer fussed over and allowed to patiently mellow like a fine wine. The world is in too much of a hurry to respect the time it takes to grow a walnut tree and to cure the blanks it yields in the air-dried tradition.

Since moisture content contributes to the stability of the stock blank, it must be carefully monitored in either the kiln or the stockmaker's attic. Between 6 and 10 percent moisture content is the desired goal. If the moisture in the blank is excessive, the finished stock will have a greater tendency to warp. Warping is the scourge of every custom stockmaker, as it can quickly sabotage the fitted dimensions built into a customer's stock. To protect their customers and their reputations, serious stockmakers are very particular about the quality of wood they select. While some of the older gun houses occasionally reach back into dusty attics for premier stock blanks that have been drying for a couple of decades or more, most of the wood supplied to the trade today spends as little as six months drying in the kiln. However, among the old guard in the stockmaker guild, the adage "The older the better" still prevails.

The stockbending jig can cure a bevy of shooting ills.

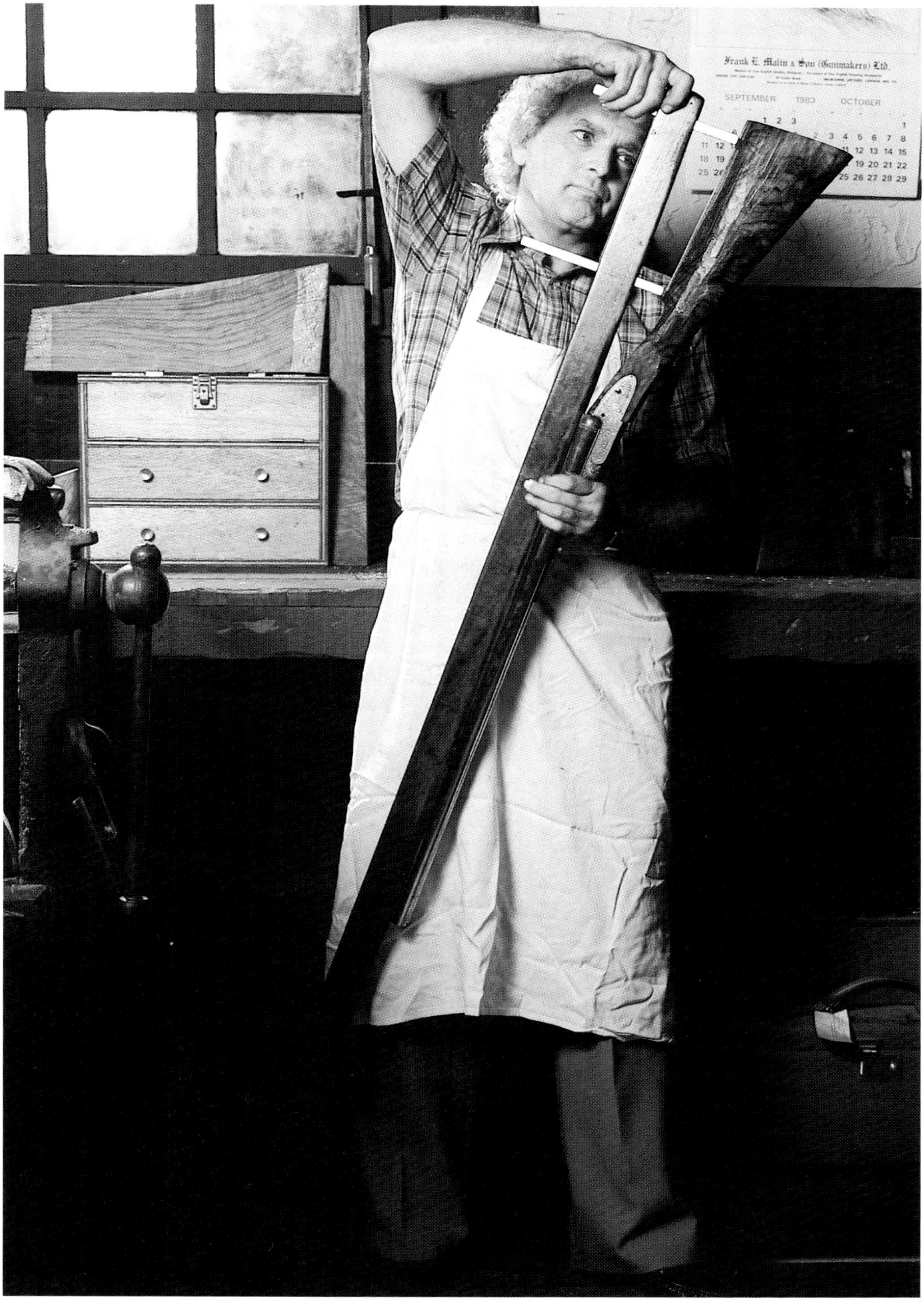
Frank E. Malin & Son (Gunmakers) Ltd.
SEPTEMBER 1983 OCTOBER

INLETTING

The overall quality of a game gun can be quickly assessed by scrutinizing the wood-to-metal fit. Improper inletting around the sidelocks, safety tang, trigger-guard strap, and fore-end fittings is a strong hint that the gunmaker has probably compromised the quality of the gun elsewhere as well. Proper inletting requires trained hand-eye coordination, extensive knowledge of woodworking tools, an understanding of gun dynamics, and a copious amount of lampblack. With the patience of a saint, the stockmaker continually applies smoke to the metal parts, presses them to the wood, and cuts away the high spots until the marriage of wood to metal is consummated.

Inletting is time-consuming, laborious work that, if pursued in the game gun tradition, must be accomplished entirely by hand. As the wood is cut away to accept the metal, it must be chiseled, filed, and sanded at a slight angle, especially around the lockplates. This tapering or chamfering type of woodcut ensures that the metal parts, when drawn up to the wood, will fit snugly, leaving no gaps. The chamfering cut is of particular importance when inletting a hand-detachable sidelock. Because the lockplates in this mechanism are often held fast to the action with a single transverse screw, the chamfering cut ensures that the locks are seated securely in place.

As the lampblack is applied to the metal and removed from the wood to provide housing for the sidelock mechanism, the jaws of the stock become a honeycomb of inletting. To maintain the structural integrity of the wood that supports the internal workings of the sidelock, clean cuts of uniform shape and depth must be executed by the stocker. Here is where the stockmaker's knowledge of wood selection pays off, as flaws in the grain around the jaws of the stock could ruin hours of tedious stockwork.

Since each stock blank is unique and exhibits characteristics all its own, the stockmaker continually sharpens his tools to maintain the subtle "feel" so critical to precision workmanship. Upon close inspection of sidelock wood-to-metal fit, one may notice a slight margin of wood around the action and lockplates. Because game guns are built to endure for generations, were the stockmakers to make the wood in these areas flush with the metal, future repair or renovation

～ Good Wood ～

Almost as intriguing as the wood he works, the stockmaker's tools must cleanly cut and shape walnut to hairline tolerances.

of the stock would be difficult. After all, a British "best" must not only survive the rigors of shooting by numerous fathers and sons, it must also withstand the competitive slings and arrows of its peers the world over.

Inletting, like most facets of gunmaking, varies in grade. Standard inletting is performed on most production-grade guns, while best-quality inletting is reserved for custom pieces. The differences are readily apparent when the two types of stockwork are compared. The best-quality inletting is both intricate and immaculate, while the standard grade hosts a few "whiskers" and rounded margins.

Inletting is always performed on actions that are in the white. During the arduous process of fitting gun parts cleanly to the wood, the stockmaker's chisels, files, and sandpaper often mar the metal. Once the inletting is complete, the action and the parts are returned to the action filer, who removes the minor scratches and grinners with a burnishing tool.

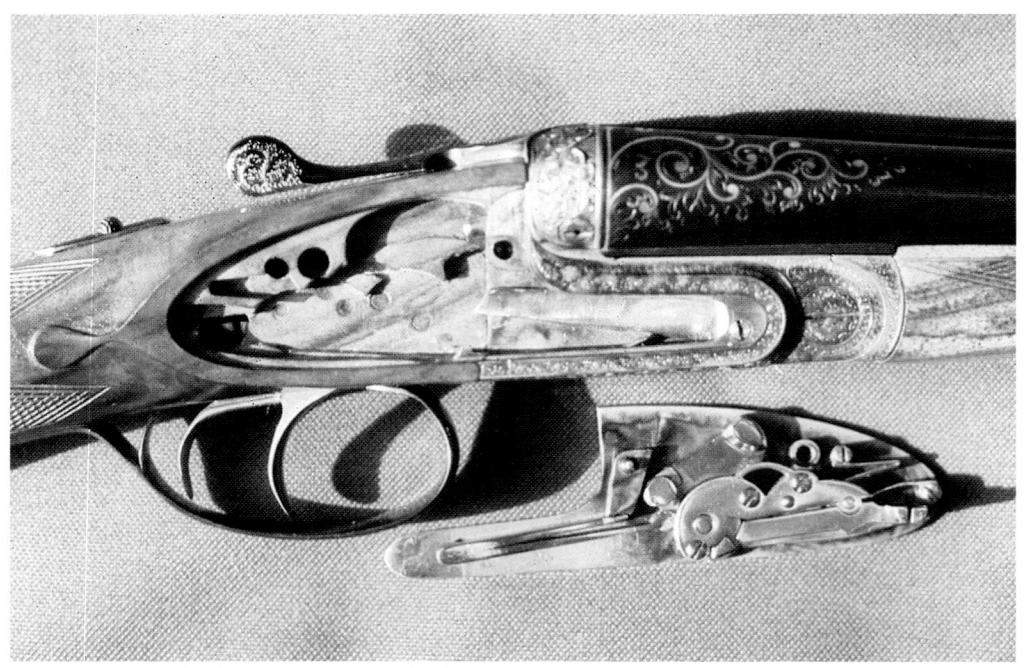

A honeycomb of inletting supports the lock mechanism of this high-grade sidelock.

STOCK CONTOURS

Those beguiling curves and contours that accentuate the heel, toe, comb, and hand of the stock are put there for purposes other than just to seduce the eye of the shooter. Custom stockmakers recognize individuality, and compensate for anatomical differences by contouring stocks that will adapt to a fleshy cheek, allow for a large hand, or respect a proud mammary gland. A bony shoulder-pocket may require a wider butt, while a buxom nimrod's stock may call for a slightly rounded toe. Comfort of fit is of paramount importance to the shooter who will mount and fire a game gun perhaps hundreds or thousands of times each season. The old "one size fits all" nemesis of mass-produced firearms is a curse that the custom stockmaker can easily cure.

For a comfortable carry afield, the size of a man's hand may dictate that the nose of the stock comb be cut back or that the circumference of the grip be increased. Such dimensions are all taken into account by the stockmaker. While some shooters may prefer a graceful oval grip at the hand, others may desire the diamond-shaped grip popularized by Holland & Holland. A myriad of stock styles and choices give the shooter an opportunity to select those features which provide the most comfort and guarantee the greatest consistency in gun mounting. These, coupled with the proper bend and cast, give the game gun shooter a distinct advantage in the field.

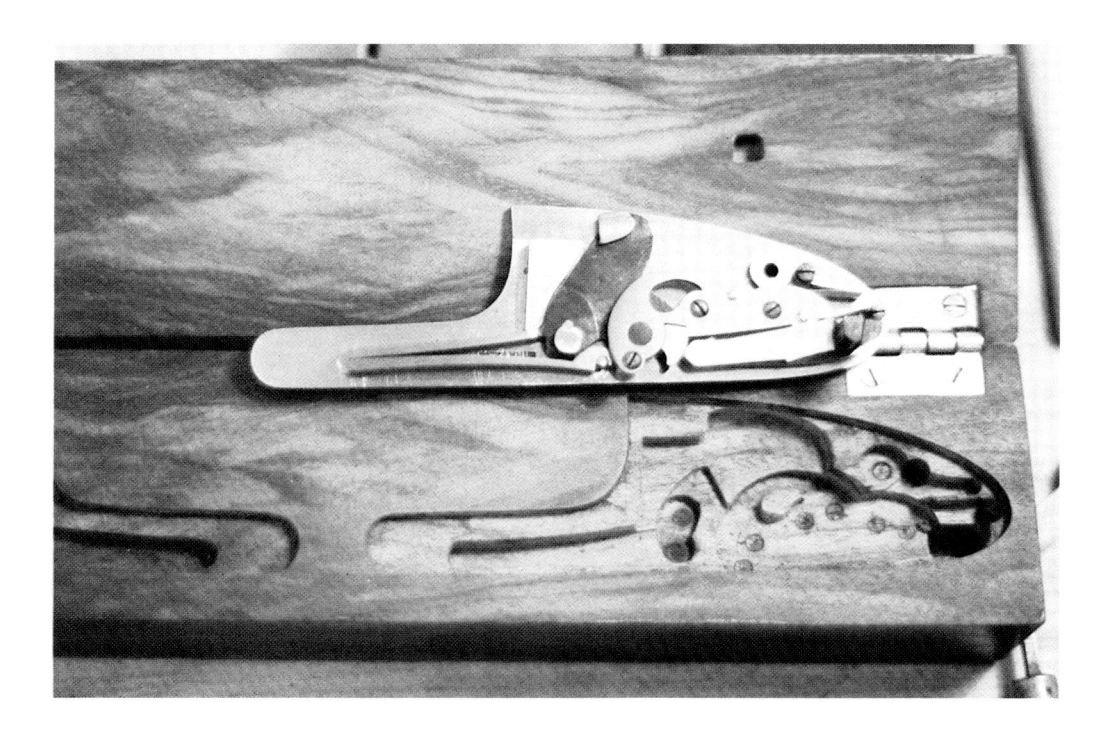

Esthetically speaking, the traditional English straight-grip stock design offers lines that have been called racy, rakish, and refined by various gun writers. Its real attraction, of course, lies not so much in its looks as it does in its function. Employing simple geometry, it is easy to see that a straight-gripped, English fore-end-fitted gun keeps the shooter's hands functioning at relatively the same level or plane. When a bird flushes, both hands must work harmoniously to serve the gun up to the shooter's line of sight. Whatever slight advantage the straight-grip gun may have over a half- (semi-) or full-pistol-grip gun is usually discovered in the violent split second of reaction time it takes to cover a flushing grouse, quail, or woodcock. And while a semi- or full-pistol grip manifests itself nicely with a beavertail fore-end and single trigger, neither adds utility to the classic game gun.

STOCK FINISHING

Once the stockmaker has completed the inletting of the metal, he must prepare the buttstock and fore-end for final finishing. Beginning with No. 100-grit (garnet) sandpaper and working down through the various grades, the stocker eventually finishes the wood with No. 400 and No. 600 wet/dry sandpaper.

Throughout the sanding process, the stockmaker is always careful to sand with the grain of the wood, especially when using the coarser grades of paper. Using various sanding blocks to hold the sandpaper securely and keep sanding margins flat, the stockmaker carefully mounts the wood in a padded vise for contouring and finishing.

Because a properly prepared work surface is critical when applying the final finish to a gunstock, the wet-dry procedure must be carried out religiously. At this stage, tap water is applied sparingly to the wood, then the stock is heated (carefully, to avoid scorching) with a gas torch to raise the grain in the wood. Some gun houses continue to use diluted oxalic acid to raise the grain more completely. These raised whiskers are sanded off, and the entire process is repeated seven or eight times until the grain is uniformly smooth throughout the stock and forearm. If this wet-dry process were overlooked or improperly done, the wood surface would become stippled and take on the texture of an orange peel during final finishing.

Out of all the finishes that can be applied to a gunstock, the London oil finish still reigns supreme in the eyes of most game gun makers. Though modern science has created synthetic finishes that can seemingly withstand satellite re-entry, to apply such substances to a classic game gun would be a little like adorning Mona Lisa's classic smile with makeup. The French polish finish remains popular in certain gun building circles, but its solution of suspended shellac leaves a high-gloss finish which is easily marred and difficult to repair or maintain.

The many organic ingredients used to concoct the oil used in a London finish are somewhat akin to a witch's brew. However, the stockmaker's caldron is usually an ordinary eight- to ten-ounce, tight-necked bottle that contains the unlikely combination of linseed oil, alkanet root, beeswax, wax polish, and paint hardener—the paint hardener being used to reduce the amount of drying time between applications. The ingredients are heated, mixed, then applied to wood surfaces with a napless cloth.

A good oil finish should penetrate the wood to a depth of at least a quarter-inch throughout. Such penetration enables small nicks and abrasions to be rubbed out with little effort.

As the passing years assault the wood, the cosmetic advantages of a London oil finish become apparent. Usually, as his last task of the day, the stockmaker spends ten minutes or so rubbing the oil treatment into the gunstock, giving it time overnight to penetrate the wood grain. First thing in the morning, he will rub in a light coat of linseed oil and apply a fine rubbing compound known as rottenstone powder. Similar in function to the rubbing compounds used to bring out the color and sheen of a car's paint finish, the rottenstone powder mellows the London oil finish to a warm radiance.

Depending on wood density, a proper London oil finish can require three weeks or more to complete. Should use afield temporarily dull the stock's sheen, a drop or two of pure linseed oil rubbed briskly into the wood will renew the glow.

Another advantage of a London oil finish is evidenced when the stock is dented. The stockmaker simply heats a specially designed iron with a gas torch and, like a magician with a wand, waves it a half inch or so above a dampened cloth placed over the dented area. If the dent is not too severe, it will be completely raised and then rubbed with rottenstone powder until it virtually disappears, all within a few short minutes. Try this with a synthetic stock finish, and a large portion, if not the entire stock, will require refinishing.

CHECKERING

Although elaborate checkering patterns can provide substantial ornamentation to a gunstock, the original purpose of wood checkering was to provide a more secure gripping surface for the shooter. On game guns, this gripping factor pertains only to the hand of the stock. The fore-end checkering is strictly cosmetic, as the shooter grasps primarily the barrels with his leading hand and not the fore-end.

While American stockmakers are particularly adept at flirting with fleur-de-lis checkering and other intricate borderless designs, the British, in typical conservative fashion, have retained the initial intent of checkering by utilizing one or two very basic designs. Aside from the carved teardrop found on the stock at the back of each lockplate, the classic lines of a straight-grip game gun do not lend themselves to fancy carving or checkering patterns. As such, English checkering is straightforward and bordered.

Over the years, much discussion has ensued concerning the number of lines per inch shotgun checkering should have. It can vary anywhere from sixteen to as many as thirty-two lines to the inch, possibly more. Presently, the makers of best-quality guns tend to prefer twenty-eight to thirty lines to the inch.

At some point, consideration should be given to the utility of such very fine checkering. Even though it may appeal to the eye and the feel of the shooter, its smaller diamonds cannot offer as much grip control as the esthetically appealing twenty-six-line checkering can provide. Some stockmakers contend that even though fine-line checkering requires more time at the bench, it is easier to produce than the coarser patterns. The reasoning behind this is that the larger the diamond, the more care must be taken to maintain its uniformity in relation to the other diamonds. Sometimes wood quality alone will dictate the number of lines per inch the checkering will carry, the coarser the wood the fewer lines per inch.

To many, traditional English checkering may appear flat and display fewer lines to the inch than one would expect on a "best" gun. However, upon closer examination of the handling dynamics of such guns, one soon discovers that the flattened diamonds enable the shooter's hand to slide smoothly along the straight grip, thus affording quick activation of the double triggers found on classic game guns. Fine checkering of twenty-eight to thirty-two lines to the inch accomplishes much the same thing, as it is more ornamental than functional and allows the hand to move more freely. Larger, flat-topped diamonds on a game gun, then, do not necessarily indicate inferior quality; this checkering design merely reflects England's two-centuries-old quest to refine and adapt game guns to the shooter's needs.

This style of checkering is not without its drawbacks. Flat checkering usually requires borders to help conceal the overruns which often result from the artisan's efforts to cut flat-topped diamonds. Though visually appealing, the flat diamonds offer little traction for shooters who prefer a more secure gripping surface. The shallow line-cuts are also easily filled with dirt and debris, further diminishing the practical and esthetic value of flat checkering. But properly maintained, English flat-checkering can retain its subtle elegance.

There are three basic tools the stockmaker uses to lay out and finish off checkering patterns: a single-line tool, a double-line tool, and a mulling or border tool.

After the outside border of the checkering pattern has been carefully drawn on the grip and fore-end, the double-line checkerer is used in leapfrog fashion across the wood. While the leading edge of this two-pronged tool cuts along the penciled border, its parallel cutting mate scribes a line at the prescribed distance alongside. This second line then becomes a guide for the leading edge of the double tool throughout the initial checkering process. Upon completing the pattern with the double-checkering tool, the stockmaker next enlists the single tool to clean and sharpen the diamonds. In order to achieve both uniform diamonds and depth of cut, the stockmaker does not bear down heavily on the tool, but merely guides it along, allowing the tool's own weight and sharp teeth to do the cutting.

Once the checkering pattern has been filled in and finished off with a single tool, then the mulling tool is brought into play to put borderlines around the checkering. This two-prong tool consists of one thick line of cutting teeth and one thin line of cutters. The thin line of teeth is placed in the outermost line of checkering, which serves as a guide for the thick line of teeth that cut the border. After the first border cut has been accomplished, the stocker reverses the wood in his vise and traces the thick teeth along the border cut, which allows the thin teeth of the tool to make a fine

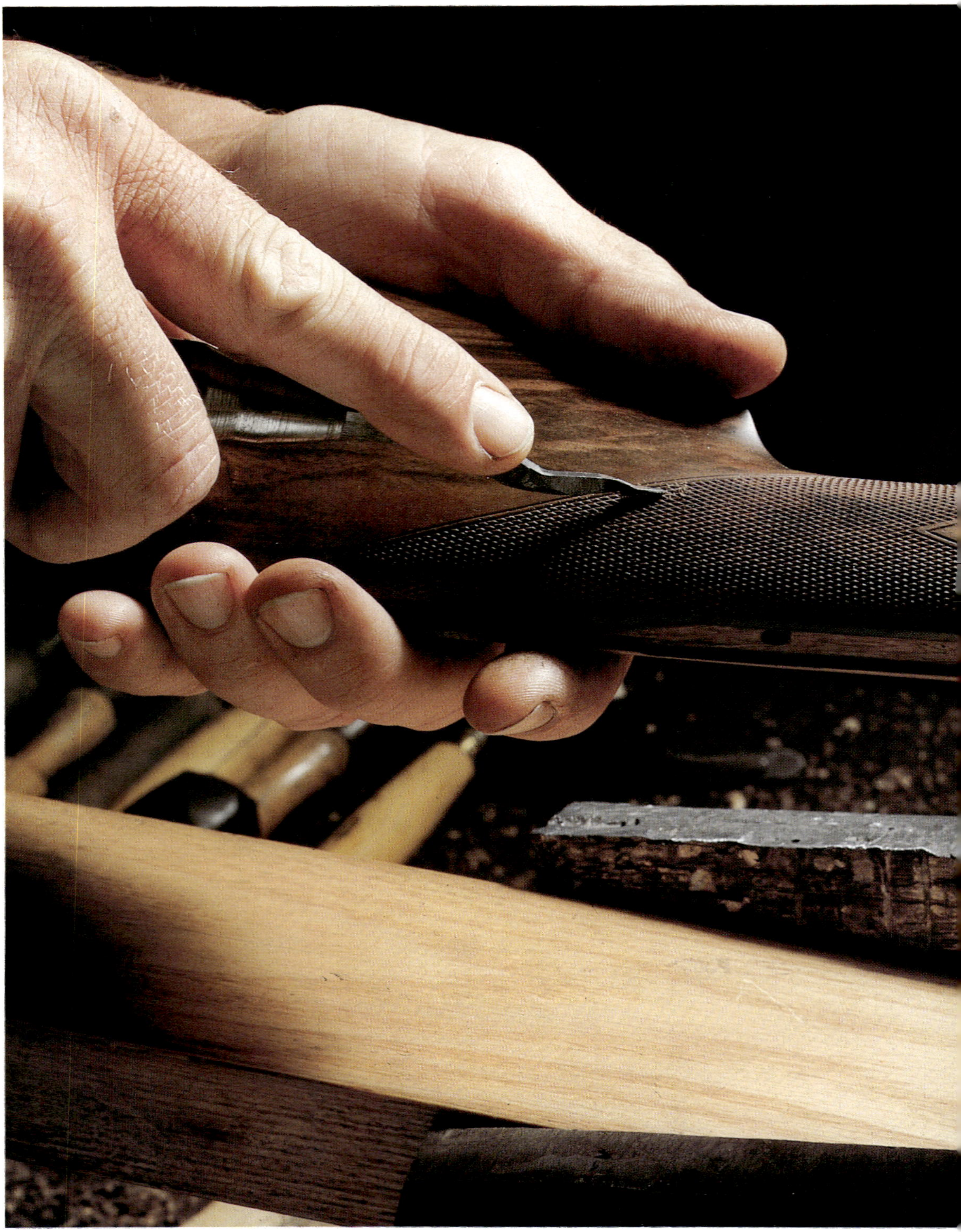

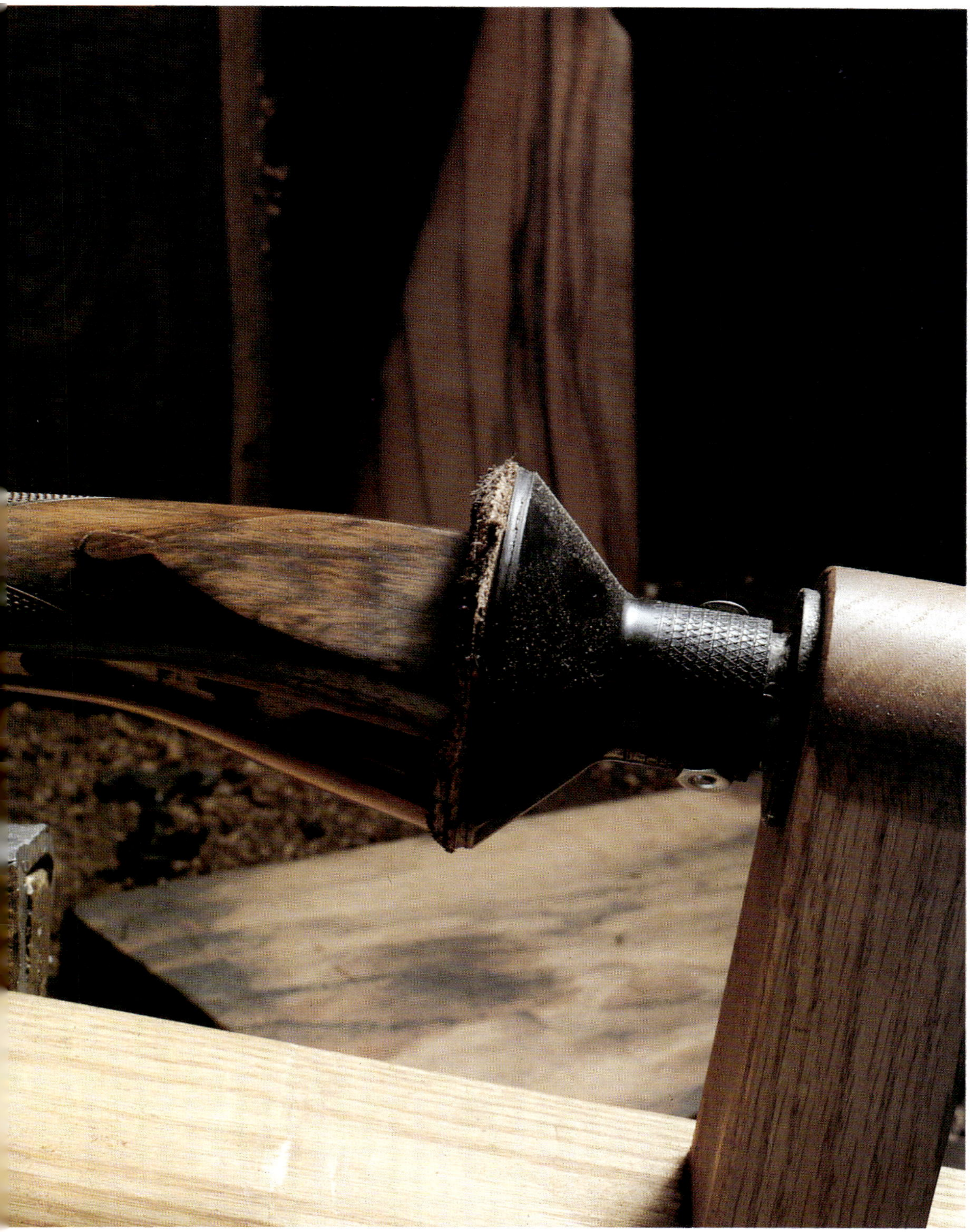

line-cut parallel to the original border. It sounds complicated, but in reality, it is very simple.

Although impressive checkering is not the English gunmaker's forte, on the higher-grade guns its execution should be as close to flawless as skilled hands can permit. Overly flattened diamonds, uneven lines, or cutting overruns belong only on a young apprentice's practicing blanks and not on any game gun of respectable grade.

Whether a stock should be checkered before or after an oil finish is applied is a matter of preference among custom stockmakers. Many houses, such as Holland & Holland, prefer to checker before the oil is applied, claiming that the wood can be cut cleaner and easier. Those who checker before applying oil also point out that accumulated debris can be quickly blown away and that the checkering tools remain sharper longer. Either way, the shooter should closely examine the finished product and judge accordingly.

TAKING STOCK

Whether silver or gold, the oval on the bottom of a game gun's buttstock originated from the thumbpiece found on flintlock pistols. Located just to the left of the pistol's barrel tang, where the shooter's thumb would naturally rest, the thumbpiece would often carry the monogram or coat of arms of the gun's owner. Early hammer guns also displayed a thumbpiece of sorts on the upper grip-section of the buttstock. However, as sporting arms gained prominence, and pride in ownership compelled gun owners to display their guns in gun cabinets, the nameplate migrated to the bottom of the buttstock. It is an accessory that, in addition to personalizing a shotgun, gives a touch of distinction to a classic game gun.

Stockmaking is not so much a mystery as it is a deep personal commitment of time, determination, and perseverance. The professional stocker constantly battles the clock as well as himself to produce the highest quality product his two hands and time will allow. Down through the years, the grand old gun houses of England have spawned master stockmakers whose work will live on long after these great craftsmen have been laid to rest.

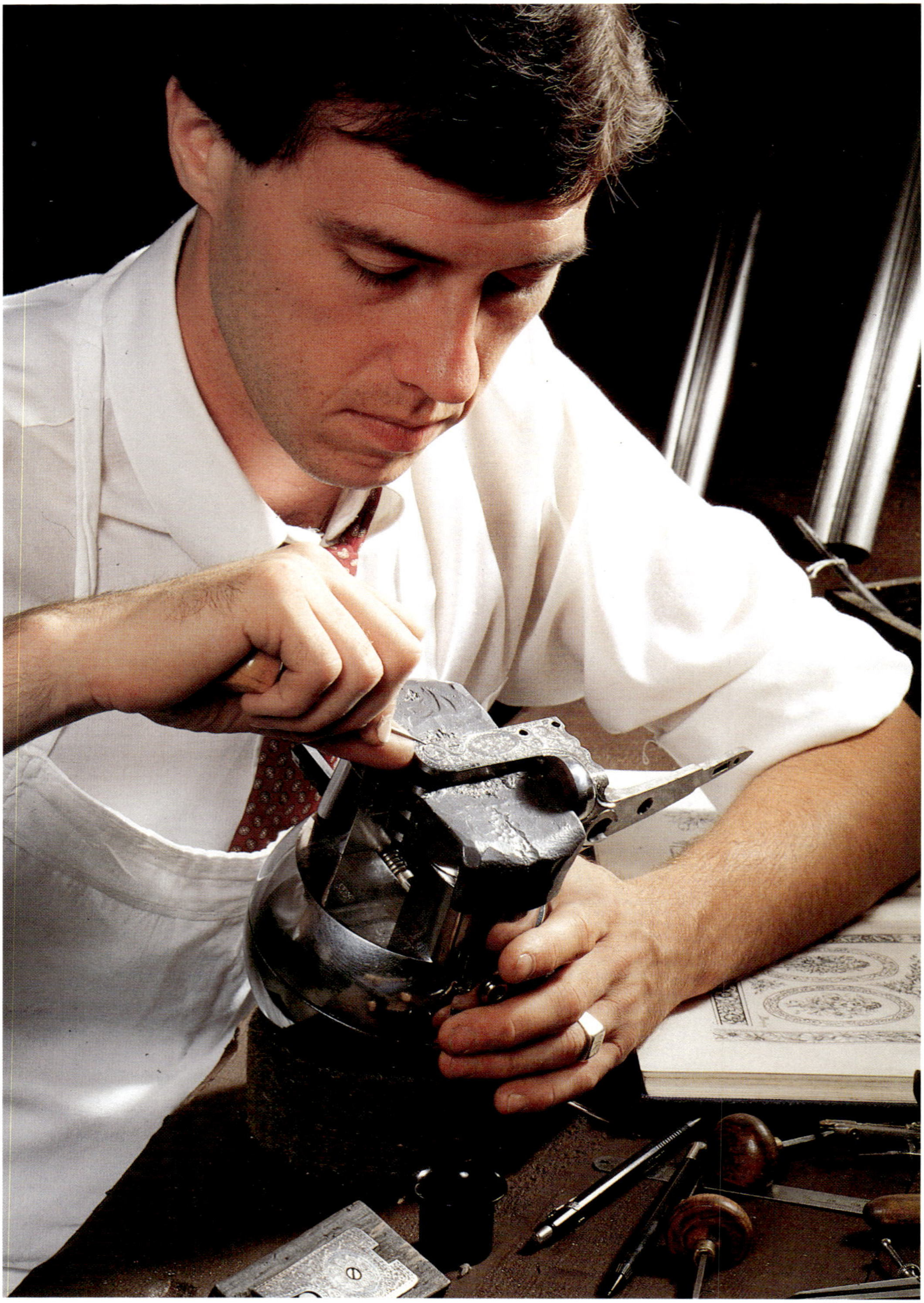

5

STEEL TAPESTRY

A<small>NCIENT ARTISANS ACROSS</small> A<small>SIA</small>, Mesopotamia, Africa, Europe, and other early cultural centers lavished engraving on wood, stone, glass, lead, bronze, and iron long before firearms steel was treated to its compelling beauty. Yet today, firearms remain the last true bastion of the engraver's art.

With each generation's rediscovery of the vitality an engraver's tools can impart to cold steel, questions arise about the evolution of new engraving techniques, styles, and patterns. Modern technology may have refined the engraver's tools, but it has done little to change the art. Engraving, applied either by machine or by hand, is ultimately guided by the centuries-old tradition of past masters who left no avenue unexplored in their pursuit of the art. Rembrandt and Whistler are but a couple of the numerous early artists whose engraving techniques would humble many of the so-called banknote master engravers today.

Contrary to popular belief, there is very little new under the sun in terms of engraving styles and patterns. The only thing contemporary man has managed to add is fancy terminology for marketing the finished product. Whether banknote, rose-and-scroll, or deep-relief, every engraving style has been explored and perfected by past masters.

Nowhere was the engraver's art pursued with more vigor than on the British Isles during the Golden Age of the English gun trade. From the early 1900s through the 1930s, many of the famous gun houses of those halcyon days exhibited a standard, everyday brand of engraving which, by contemporary standards, would be heralded as extraordinary. There remain but a handful of English engravers whose talent with a hand graver can compare with their numerous, less-exalted predecessors. Many a master engraver passed into oblivion with only his unsigned work giving silent tribute to his consummate ability. As much as it may depress the memory of England's past engraving masters, it appears now as if only those names ending in "I" are capable of such compelling metal tapestry on a production basis.

Engraving endures in the gun trade because it is the classic response to hand-held art. Game guns are the medium for the expression of graven images that animate the steel, making it more compatible with the glowing warmth of highly figured walnut. There are those who feel that engraving is a needless embellishment that, regardless of quality, is applied only to justify the gunmaker's hefty fee. These same individuals, I'll wager, wouldn't be caught in public in an automobile that didn't sport at least a little chrome trim or custom paint striping.

Like beauty, engraving is also entirely in the eye of the beholder. There are those who feel that if the sweep and curl of rose-and-scroll engraving cannot withstand the scrutiny of the jeweler's glass, it is a blight on the gun. However, certain styles of engraving come alive at arm's length, much in the same fashion that a fine impressionistic painting evokes beauty when viewed from the proper distance. Often, perfectly executed engraving of uniform depth and coverage can flatten and detract from a gun's overall appearance. When applied to gun steel without benefit of an artist's discerning eye, engraving can also become sterile, accentuating the metal's innate coldness.

Much to the chagrin of master craftsmen, modern technology has embraced the engraver's art with electric hand gravers (gravermeisters), pantograph machines, acid etching, photo etching, machine-rolled engraving, etc. For cost efficiency's sake, most firearms manufacturers have succumbed to the unfeeling precision and mirrored duplication of such impersonal engraving techniques. And while there still exists a cadre of talented engravers in this country and abroad, their output is limited primarily to piecework on a custom basis. With United States gunmakers rushing to foreign shores to mass produce their wares, little incentive exists for apprentice engravers in today's gun trade.

It is unfortunate indeed that today's double-gun fancier must pay custom prices for standard production-grade guns of obsolete manufacturers such as Baker, Fox, L. C. Smith, Lefever, and others. But that which is past is also prologue, and the future no doubt holds a few trump cards for the U.S. gunmaker with the right kind of grit and high-tech know-how who can efficiently combine the best of the old with the best of the new and to create a high quality, reasonably priced double gun.

There is no more affluent consumer than the American sportsman. Given a proper education on the intrinsic value of the side-by-side double gun, with a sweetening dash of romance and marketing savvy, many an American shotgunner will set aside his trusty repeater and make room for a solidly built and tastefully engraved double gun.

In England, the renowned gun houses have always strived to maintain a stable of skilled engravers despite the slackening demand for high-grade game guns in recent years. Unfortunately, the attrition rate among apprentice gun engravers is relatively high. Often enticed by the outward serenity and cleanliness of the engraving room, young hopefuls soon discover that it takes considerable stamina in addition to artistic talent to make the grade. Practicing on plates of brass with hand gravers, the apprentice must first display a grasp of the basic engraving strokes before advancing to gun steel. Depending on his ability to learn, an artisan who graduates from brass spends a great deal of time engraving pins (screw heads), often a tedious and frustrating task. Many a pin is filed to a nubbin by the apprentice before any degree of competence is achieved.

Once the basic scroll patterns are mastered, the apprentice usually begins engraving standard-grade boxlock guns, fore-end furniture, trigger guards, opening levers, etc. It is not unusual for a fledgling engraver in some of the more conservative gun houses to spend several years producing the same rose-and-scroll patterns. A very limited few advance to master status where more creativity and self-expression is allowed. While presently there is no dearth of custom engravers, the inviolate law of diminishing supply and demand has so sapped the gun trade that custom-quality engraving on production-grade guns may soon become history.

Like gifted surgeons, fine engravers possess an almost uncanny gift of hand-eye coordination that they continually refine with each new work they complete. However, as with any worthwhile trade or profession, an engraver is only as good as his tools, and hand tools are highly coveted in the gun trade. Stories abound among engravers

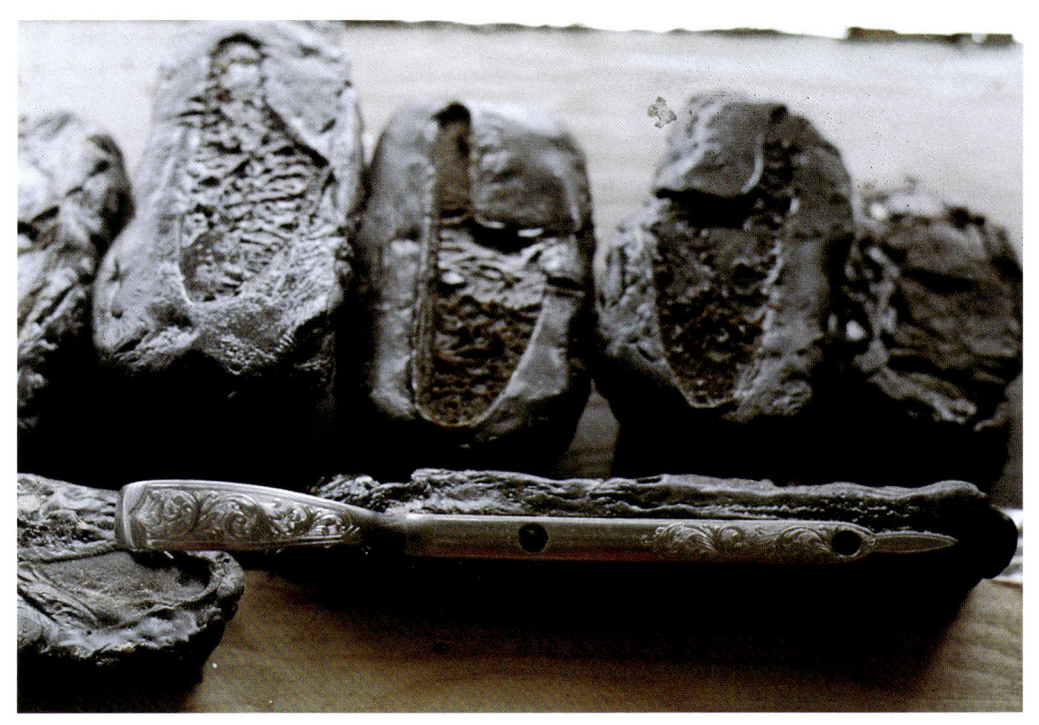

A staple of the old gun trade, engraver's pitch cradles the metal parts, holding them fast in a resilient cushion while the engraver plies his craft.

about younger craftsmen all but stumbling over a fallen old master's cooling corpse to seize a prized instrument crucial to some esoteric phase of game gun manufacture. Often, such tools are as much a work of art as the guns for which they were created. Most of these hand tools are shaped and honed to personal preferences by the engraver. Surprisingly, even some of the most intricate and compelling engraving is accomplished with a few very simple tools.

First and foremost in the engraver's arsenal is the single-stroke shader, which is used for cutting single lines. The "specker" is another English hand tool that is used to flick out the fine details inside the scrollwork of rose-and-scroll engraving. An engraving tool universal to the gun trade is the chasing chisel. Directed by blows from a small toffee hammer, the chasing chisel cuts the outside shape of the scroll's curl. Many old-timers in the English gun trade still refer to this tool as a "punch," causing no end of confusion among continentals who know a punch as something to apply lettering or proof marks to gun steel.

Used to properly design, space, and balance engraving patterns, calipers are indispensable instruments to the engraver. Many of today's engravers attain symmetry in their engraving by lifting a pattern from one side of the action and transferring it to the opposite side with cellophane and talcum powder or similar substances. In this fashion, balance is achieved without a great deal of comparative checking and handling of the action body.

Engravers from the Golden Age of game gun making would be quick to point out that, in spite of the many metallurgical advances spawned by contemporary science, the metal used in the trade during those bygone days exhibited a much better standard of cut than today's gun steel. This was not because it was necessarily softer, but because it was of a structure and uniformity that enabled the engraver to approach each new gun, regardless of which batch of steel it came from, in the same way. Unfortunately, such

With hammer and punch (metal chisel) in hand, the engraver cuts a bead around the fences.

metal consistency is rarely found in modern gun steel, requiring today's engraver to be more flexible in adapting his style to each gun engraved.

Steel hardness to an engraver is more a matter of feel than anything else. Actually, hardness and softness of steel are entirely relative terms. Since many engravers tend to be sinewy and slight in build (as compared to burly-chested action filers and long-armed barrel strikers), their sensitivity to gun steel is acute. Because their tools require a blend of art, geometry, and manual dexterity, engravers must demand more of themselves than the gun steel they strive to accentuate. Whether the steel feels too soft or diamond hard, it is a medium that master engravers must learn to control if any measure of consistency is to be achieved. Most engravers would tend to agree that metal annealed to a claylike softness is very difficult to cut. The tool has a tendency to sink into such metal, often preventing the engraver from making sharp, clean strokes.

Barrels are prepared for engraving (top). Hand graver traces fine English scroll (bottom).

Though a blessing to today's cost-conscious gunmaker, investment-cast gun steel can be a curse to the engraver. Receivers made by this lost-wax process, although faithful in every detail to the original mold, can exhibit vagaries in the steel that can exasperate even the most skilled engraver. Randomly hard and soft, not unlike Damascus layers of iron, cast steel often inhibits the engraver from making fluid, uniform strokes. Such metal inconsistency can raise hob with fine English scroll engraving. It can also produce a corrugated visual effect in the finished engraving that can detract from the lines of the gun.

Game gun engraving cannot be approached from simply the engraver's point of view. The master engraver will consider many aspects before applying graver to steel. First and foremost, he must study the action body shape and other lines of the gun. Were he to mount a sideplate in the engraver's pitch and leg vise without regard for the total gun, the engraved result could detract from the overall integrity of the piece. Engraver's pitch, by the way, is a coal by-product with a consistency similar to sealing wax. It is still used by old-timers in the trade to cradle and secure the part being engraved. When heated with a torch, it becomes pliable and can be shaped to hold sideplates, fore-end iron, etc., firmly. Many engravers believe that the pitch's resilient nature serves as a cushion for the small but powerful strokes they must make to bring vitality to fine English scroll. The leg vise is another disappearing vestige of the old gun trade, its demise hastened by the appeal and acceptance of the universal tilt vise introduced by jewelry engravers.

Whatever an engraver may think about the beauty and essence of engraving as an art form, if he prides himself as a gun engraver,

A world-class engraver is often a master of many arts and skills, from inlaid game scenes (above) and deep relief scroll engraving (page 102) to fine scroll and "bulino" (banknote) game scenes (left). Engraving and photo (above) courtesy of Winston Churchill.

he cannot wander far from the form and function of a game gun. Although dedicated in his efforts to satisfy every customer's whims, a good game-gun engraver will have second thoughts about engraving scenes on sideplates that have little if anything to do with hunting. Dragsters, locomotives, oil wells, and Roman goddesses of the hunt can all be worked onto gun metal, but the hunter will be hard pressed to find an open season on any of these. It borders on sacrilege to engrave such objects on a shotgun which is destined for the game fields.

In addition to fine English rose-and-scroll (which has a seemingly universal appeal when carefully applied to sidelocks and boxlocks), engraving patterns on a game gun should celebrate the game species most prized by the hunter. Wildfowlers and upland bird hunters pursue a wide array of birds from which the engraver can choose.

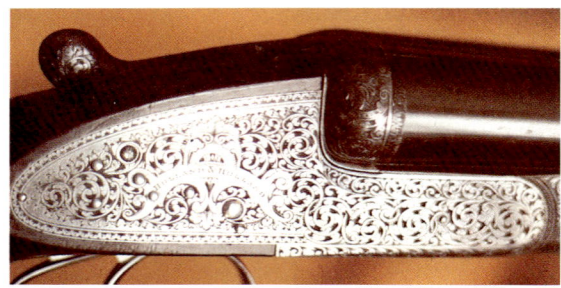

The variations of scroll engraving border on the infinite, limited only by the skill and imagination of the engraver. However, for simplicity's sake, there are two basic scroll engraving techniques from which all the variations are spawned. First there is a single-stroke fine scroll which means simply that the stroke within the scroll is achieved with a single stroke. These single strokes are repeated concentrically as the engraver builds upon his scrollwork pattern. This type of scroll engraving was applied primarily to production-grade guns and is considered a "cheap" version of fine scroll by the trade.

The second style of fine English scroll, reserved for best-quality guns, is referred to as "drop spec" fine scroll. This engraving style consists of an initial light stroke followed by a heavy drop spec cut into the back of the primary stroke. It is from these two basic patterns, then, that the engraver can launch into a myriad of scroll variations, such as open cutaway scroll, deep cutaway scroll, heavy carving, etc.

As popular as English rose-and-scroll has remained among game gun enthusiasts, banknote engraving, or "bulino," has brought a gleam to the eyes of a new generation of shotgunners. Properly executed, bulino engraving can realistically portray an endless variety of sporting motifs. Before photo-plating was developed, the printing industry relied heavily on the banknote engraving process for its printing plates.

Simple hand gravers are once again employed by the master engraver to apply the subtle light and dark shading cuts that create a photograph-like image on the metal surface. An old art form, bulino has reached its highest status in Italy, and many of the fine game guns built in that country are treated to its dramatic visual effect. Some engravers have successfully combined English rose-and-scroll with banknote game scenes to give game guns a truly museum-quality appearance. However, concern has been expressed by a few veteran engravers that bulino lends itself to fraudulent reproduction via the photo etching process. It is claimed that an original banknote design can be easily acid etched (in mass production fashion) onto shotgun sideplates. Whether true or not, it would take a well-trained eye to detect such clever forgery due to the photographic-like quality of bulino.

Because the quality of engraving tends to reflect the quality of a game gun, gunmakers are continually striving to embellish their wares with breathtaking examples of the engraver's art. From Parker's first Invincible to Holland & Holland's Chatsworth gun, the goal is always the same: unparalleled quality. After nearly two centuries of game gun refinement, getting a leg up on one's competition is no easy task. As such, gunmakers pull out all stops to create guns that will catch the public's eye.

One such gun which caught my attention is a rather radically engraved piece named the "Woodcock Gun," which was built in London by John Wilkes and engraved by Malcolm Appleby. The Woodcock Gun is a sidelock side-by-side whose action and sideplates are engraved almost entirely in woodcock plumage. Were its composition and execution any less perfect, its bold departure from the norm would have only garnered it disregard among master craftsmen and the shooting public. An engraved effigy of a noble game bird, the Woodcock Gun truly represents another forward step among engravers to capture the extraordinary on steel.

The art of inlaying precious metal into gun steel has existed for centuries. Gold and silver continue to grace the barrels and receivers of high-quality game guns world-wide. Gold on a sporting arm is a moot point in many shooter/collector circles, with the more conservative considering it garish, needless ornamentation, while their counterparts argue that tasteful gold inlays enhance the beauty of a double gun. The methods for wedding soft metal to hard steel vary from one gunmaker to the next, but there are a few basic techniques common to all.

Gold is most often used in conjunction with game-scene engraving to accentuate various game animals and sporting dogs. It can, along with silver, also be used as a borderline for scroll and game-scene engraving. Game animals remain the predominant choice of classic gunmakers, or gold inlay work, ranging from Africa's "big five" (elephant, lion, leopard,

Gold inlay is meticulous and time-consuming work. After preparing the work surface the engraver cuts a deep relief pattern in the fence, cuts a corresponding pattern out of 24-karat gold, and with a single blow hammers it into place.

Before any of the precious metal can be inlaid, the gun steel must first be engraved and bevel-cut to receive the gold. This Browning Superposed was beautifully upgraded by the renowned master engraver Winston Churchill.

The Lesson

cape buffalo, and rhino, found on double rifles) to North America's waterfowl and upland birds.

Prior to receiving the gold inlay, the gun steel must be carefully prepared by the engraver. The working surface must be burnished free of grinners, and degreased. The desired design is then drawn in detail onto the steel with a pencil. Once this is achieved, the engraver begins to cut the steel within the design to a uniform depth of about $1/32$ of an inch. In order for the steel to accept and hold a raised gold inlay, a reverse bevel (dovetail) cut must be made around the outline of the design.

Next, the engraver draws and cuts an exact duplicate of the design from a sheet of 24-karat gold (usually 10- to 18-karat for game guns destined for rigorous work afield). The gold design is then placed on the steel cutout and struck solidly with an appropriately sized

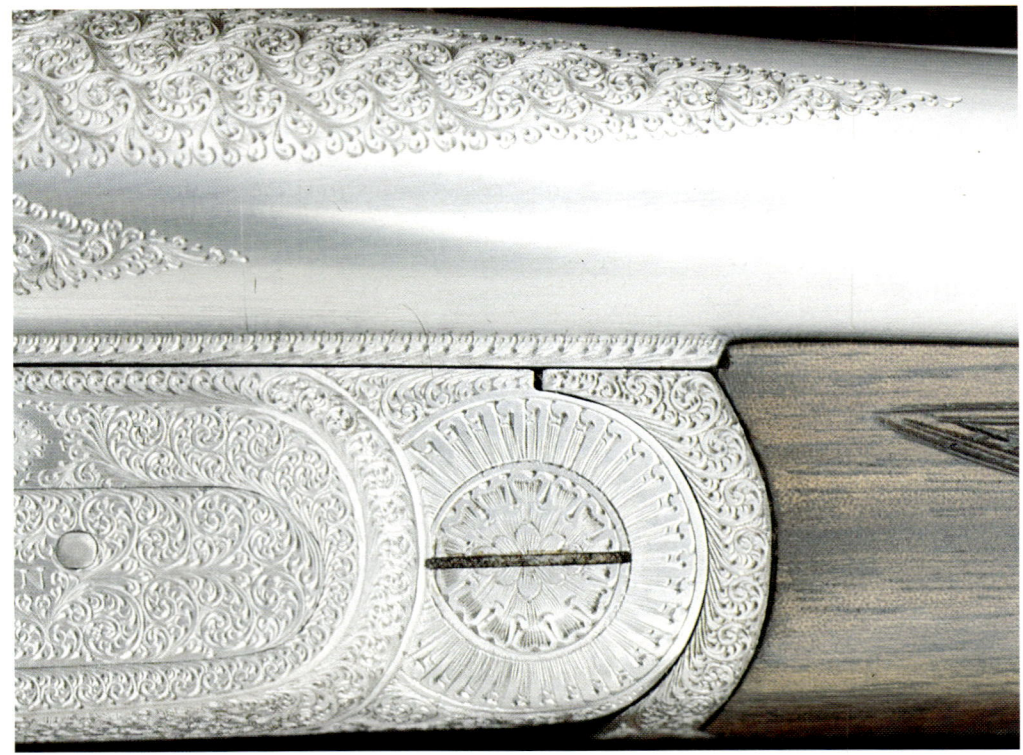

Still "in the white," this barreled action exhibits fine English rose-and-scroll engraving at its best.

Open cutaway scroll requires even more time and attention from the engraver.

punch and hammer. The Lord willing, and if luck prevails, the gold will expand laterally into the bevel cuts and hold fast for a generation or two. To finish the inlay, the engraver carves back the gold to its original dimension and redefines the anatomy of the game animal. Every raised gold inlay must be prepared in this manner.

A flat gold inlay is achieved in much the same way, but the steel cut is shallower and the anatomical detail is engraved after the gold is punched in place, filed flat, cut back, and polished.

Another gold inlay method used in the trade is the overlay. Again, the game-animal design is drawn on the receiver, lock plate, or barrel of the shotgun. Using a flat-ended chisel, the engraver scores the design at an angle with a series of bevel cuts, then, in a method not unlike wood checkering, cuts across the design from the opposite angle. The gold cutout is positioned on the serrated surface and given a sharp blow with a steel punch and hammer. This overlay method gives the engraver considerable flexibility in designing the game animal or scene, but it does have one very disturbing drawback: the inlay has a greater tendency to part company with the gun under stressful shooting conditions.

Gold, silver, and even porcelain have graced the fences and frames of double guns for centuries. If applied discreetly, inlays can enhance the appearance of fine shotguns. However, most purists tend to agree that a game gun properly engraved with rose-and-scroll does not lack for embellishment.

As compelling as fine English scroll and tasteful gold inlay work can be, high-class deep-relief engraving can also add a dramatic dimension to game gun design. This style of engraving (not to be confused with the inferior-quality work often produced by hand-held machines) is achieved with the same basic tools used in fine scroll engraving, with greater emphasis on the use of the chasing chisel. Four different styles of chasing chisels, a liner tool (engraving chisel), a single punch stippler, and hand gravers are all employed by the artist to carve the deep-relief designs found on many high-grade double guns.

By its very nature, deep-relief engraving is a very time-consuming task. When the metal is chiseled away from around the scrollwork, the original engraving design is nicked and blemished and must be cleaned up by the engraver. Unfortunately, when the background is stipple punched, the engraving design is once again slightly marred and must be reworked. Once this has been achieved, the engraver cuts in the highlights around the scrollwork to further detail and accent the engraving pattern. As a result, even a simple-looking deep-relief design often requires the same amount of time to complete as a more intricate rose-and-scroll pattern.

A classic example of high-class deep-relief engraving can be seen on vintage Holland & Holland Royal Grade shotguns, those built in the 1920s and '30s. Its style was very delicate and understated, but its esthetic effects on the lines of the gun are quite obvious. By comparison today, there exist a number of European gun houses whose

Engraving and photo courtesy Winston Churchill.

deep-relief engraving approaches the early Holland & Holland quality and, from a production volume standpoint, can be considered the standard-bearers of the contemporary gun trade.

Whether engraved with fine English rose-and-scroll, deep-relief game scenes, gold inlays, or a combination of each, a "best" game gun takes an accomplished engraver from two to three weeks to complete. When asked how long it took him to engrave a sidelock gun, one engraver said in a serious tone, "All my life." Considering the years of apprenticeship and additional time spent experimenting and perfecting skills, it indeed takes a talented artisan all his life to engrave a best-quality game gun.

If, from a purely esthetic standpoint, high-quality engraving adds nothing more than pride of ownership to a game gun, it is in keeping with the great tradition of the hunt. Such embellishment symbolizes the ritual and recognition that hunters have always given game animals and hunting tools. And while the tide of engraving consensus will continue to ebb and flow, one thing will always remain constant among those who still demand the best: the quest for perfection.

L. C. Smith Crown Grade Long Range. Photo by William W. Headrick, courtesy of Lewis Drake & Associates.

6

AMERICAN MADE

THE OLD DOUBLE HAD A WORN PATINA on its stock and steel that spoke of seasons of service in the game fields. Its fluid steel barrels were long and gracefully tapered, showing a hint of case wear and a small dent near the muzzle of the right tube. The checkering on the splinter forearm was a faint shadow of its original sharp-pointed diamonds of twenty-four lines to the inch. Its buttstock was lightly scarred from repeated encounters with brambles, briars, and underbrush.

Though used, the double-triggered gun had not been abused. The external screw heads on the receiver and the pistol-grip tang were in proper alignment and showed no signs of careless tampering. Its triggers were crisp, its locks responsive, and its bolting solid. Its ejectors were also well timed and regulated. The opening lever was still slightly right of center, and no sliver of light could be seen when I silhouetted the closed breech against the building's skylight.

Forged and fabricated in the face of America's longest depression, the old gun reflected the same strength of character that enabled a nation to endure the worst of times. It was truly an "Old Reliable." I admired the dog-head buttplate, its checkered Bakelite polished smooth by countless trips to the shoulder.

"Give me twelve hundred," the gun trader barked, breaking my silent inspection of the American icon I held snugly against my shoulder. The old boy knew I was more than a casual observer; he was a veteran of the gun-show circuit and was working me with all the savvy of a well-trained bird dog working quail.

Without taking my eyes off of the gun I knew I would be taking home, I asked if he would take $900. He slowly stroked his salt-and-pepper beard and leaned back against his chair. "That's a rare Parker, ya won't find very many 16s on an O frame," he countered. I nonchalantly laid the DHE back on the table. It was the only Parker he had, but it was in good company. Spread out on both sides of the gun were samples of some of America's finest shotguns—a Monogram L. C. Smith, two XE-Grade Foxes, an Optimus Lefever, a Baker Paragon, a gold-inlaid Winchester Model 21 duck, and a pair of Ithaca 4-E doubles. Each gun harkened back to a time when quality was as much a part of America as television and aspirin are today.

I was admiring them all when the wizened collector said with a touch of surrender in his voice, "Son, if ya got a thousand dollars in your pocket, the Parker's yours." I lightened my wallet and never looked back.

Over the years, as gun shows came and went, I would occasionally find the old gun collector seated stoically behind his table educating the space-age generation about the beautiful hand-built guns he offered. Each time I saw him, he displayed fewer and fewer of his well-kept relics. I sometimes believe he was reluctant to sell his treasures from the past to the modern shooting public, who understood repeaters and over-unders better than they understood side-by-sides. I learned a lot about shotgun craftsmanship from the old man and the Parker; both he and the gun were a part of a sporting heritage that spawned some of America's finest outdoor experiences and writing.

America's melting pot offered its gunmakers a labor force whose work ethic was based, in large part, on strict Old World standards. The diversity of cultural backgrounds converged in such gunmaking cities as Philadelphia, Pennsylvania; Meriden, Connecticut; New Haven, Connecticut; Ilion, New York; Ithaca, New York; Bowling Green, Ohio; and others.

Much of the engraving found on high-grade American guns was produced by artisans of English extraction. The scroll engraving especially has a characteristic English sweep and curl. Because of the demand by American sportsmen, most of the doubles were game-scene engraved. In the lower grades, the engraved gun dogs, woodcock, quail, and other game were often crude caricatures in comparison to today's bulino-engraved game scenes. However, America's top-of-the-line doubles exhibited a quality of engraving and gold-inlay work that is equaled today by only a handful of engravers.

While white-collared WASPs buzzed around the front offices of America's gun firms keeping the financial machinery on track, metalworkers and stockers from Russia, Poland, Czechoslovakia, Germany, and Ireland sweated through their aprons behind punch presses, grinding wheels, drill presses, and other gunmaking machinery. As diverse as the parts of the gun, these workers combined their sweat and pride to create guns that were as unique as the American dream that spawned them both. From 1830 to 1930, America's immigrants built the greatest country in the history of the world. America's sporting arms were symbolic of the courage, determination, and ingenuity that forged a nation out of the frontier.

If you are fortunate enough to ever own one or more of America's classic side-by-sides, the following is dedicated to you and to the thinning ranks of old men who cared enough about quality to create some of the best shotguns money could buy. With some loving care and prudent gunsmithing, most of America's finer old double guns can be restored to the game fields for a few more generations; the guns deserve such treatment as much as a new generation of hunters needs to treat itself to America's best.

"OLD RELIABLE": THE PARKER

Just after the Civil War, Charles Parker introduced a sporting double gun that set a standard of quality for the entire nation. For nearly seventy-five years, the Parker name was synonymous with quality and reliability. The name, like the gun, is as solid today as it was in the good old days. Of the 200,000-plus guns produced by Parker, nearly half were built with Damascus twist barrels. In fact, the graceful sweep and figure of the Damascus tubes were so popular that they endured for nearly two decades after fluid steel barrels and smokeless powder were introduced.

Anyone contemplating hunting with one of these vintage Parkers is tempting fate. Age robs Damascus steel barrels of what little structural integrity they may have had in the first place. There are those who will boast of the many rounds of trap or skeet they have shot with Grandpa's Damascus double and modern clay target loads. The dynamics of Damascus are such that most tubes frequently burst in the proximity of the shooter's leading hand. As fond as I am of the

Parker DHE Grade 20-gauge. Photo by William W. Headrick, courtesy of Lewis Drake & Associates.

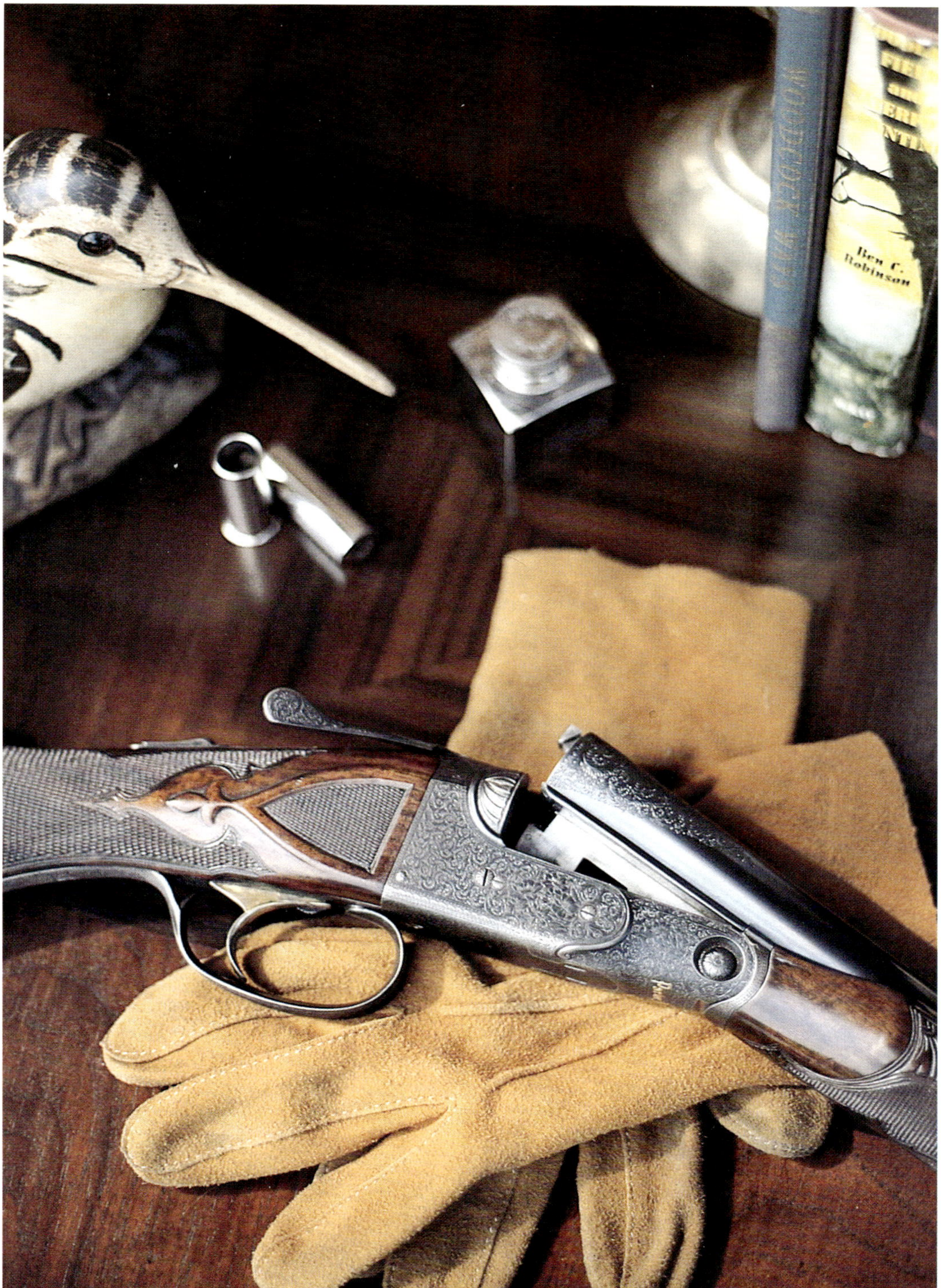
Ben C.
Robinson

nostalgia and charm these old guns offer, I cherish my anatomy a great deal more.

Some hunters have tried to resurrect the shootability of these shotguns by placing barrel inserts of a lesser gauge down their tubes. What such inserts may add in terms of shootability, they subtract from the gun's overall balance and feel. A better, albeit more costly, alternative would be to have a competent gunsmith amputate the Damascus barrels to within $3\frac{1}{4}$ inches of the breech and sleeve the remaining unit with fluid steel tubes; this procedure was introduced and perfected by Westley Richards of England in the late 1950s.

The process is really quite simple. The breech section is bored out and, after grinding, the new steel barrels (which extend through to the breech face) are shrink soldered into the original breech section. The gunsmith then strikes off the new tubes so that they blend in with the original breech, replaces the original ribs where possible, and blacks the barrels.

Properly sleeved, the shotgun can now handle modern loads safely, and the sleeving joint is seldom perceptible after the barrels are rust-blued. To further hide the repair, some gunmakers engrave the sleeving joint. Because most Damascus-barreled guns made by Parker and other gun companies were usually thirty to thirty-four inches long (for complete combustion of black-powder loads), the sleeving process allows the hunter to select shorter tube lengths, more in keeping with upland bird hunting requirements. However, some stock hollowing may be required to balance the shorter barrels.

Parker's simple bolting mechanism was improved during the early 1900s with the addition of a tapered combination bolt plate that automatically compensated for wear. It would be prudent for the hunter desiring to restore a Parker for bird shooting to have this bolt plate installed. Not only will it improve the strength of the gun, but it will guarantee trouble-free and secure bolting for many seasons afield.

The DelGrego Family of Ilion, New York, has all the parts and expertise needed to transform the bolting mechanism on older Parkers. They also have the tools and know-how to remedy Parker's intricate and touchy ejector system. It is not unusual to find used Parkers whose ejectors are out of synchronization and in need of timing and regulation. This task is better left to someone who has intimate experience with the ejector idiosyncrasies of the Parker gun. The DelGregos have two generations of such experience and were always recommended highly for repair work by the late Charles S. Parker, grandson of the company's founder.

Either by circumstance or by fate, all the Parkers I have owned had barrels that were dented or bulged to some degree. Most of the dents were minor and would not affect the quality of the

Parker's A-1 Special reflects a quality of craftsmanship that galvanized its reputation as one of the world's best-made shotguns. See also page 119.

patterns thrown by the guns. But there is something about looking through a shiny barrel and seeing a shadowy interruption of the light rings that disturbs me.

The 16-gauge I bought from the gun collector was one such gun. The small dent in its right barrel taunted me every time I inspected the barrels. Repairing barrel dents or bulges is really not as mysterious as it may seem. When I sent this gun to the DelGregos, I asked them to outline their procedure for removing barrel dents. The procedure is as ingenious as it is simple: progressively larger steel plugs are tapped through the bore to expand the dent. As each plug enters the dented area, the gunsmith stress-relieves the exterior of the barrel around the dent with a brass hammer. After the dent is completely reduced, the barrel is rebored to eliminate interior tool marks. In preparation for rust-bluing, the barrels are carefully re-struck and carded (sanded) to preserve margins, engraving, and other barrel markings. Barrel dents are all in a day's work for the competent gunsmith, but because of the rust-bluing process, the entire procedure can take upwards of two weeks to be completed.

Because Parker ejectors can be troublesome to repair, at no time should the hunter dry-fire his double and allow the ejectors to snap on empty chambers. Parkers are fitted with rebounding hammers, so the dry-firing will not harm the firing mechanism, but the kicking ejectors can damage the ejector stop built into the doll's-head barrel extension. The use of snap caps is recommended to protect firing pins and ejectors during dry-firing. If no snap caps or empty hulls are available, Parker owners can prevent damage to the ejector stop by allowing the ejectors to kick against their thumb. It can smart a little, but not as much as the bill for repairing the doll's-head stop.

A shooter can also determine the extent of use a black-powder Parker has received by examining the amount of pitting on the standing breech around the firing pin holes. Black-powder shotshells were made with corrosive primers and have left their caustic tracks on the standing breech of many a fine old gun. Seldom does the pitting erode the breech to the point where bushings must be installed, but for cosmetic purposes, bushings eliminate the unsightly scars. Usually, the pitting will be heaviest around the right firing pin hole, the barrel most often fired.

Another price which must be paid by the hunter who wants to shoot a turn-of-the-century Parker or similar relic is that of recoil effect. Chambers for these old guns were reamed to accommodate cartridges with thicker brass rims and heads than today's modern ammunition. The difference results in some head-spacing problems that manifest themselves in a bit more felt recoil and distorted brass. The shooter can test for this by simply placing unfired shells into the gun and gently rocking the barrels up and down. The tapping of the cartridges against the standing breech can easily be heard. Unless the hunter is a hopeless purist, demanding no play, rattles, or other imperfections in his guns, the head-spacing problem is inconsequential to the joy of hunting with an American legacy. Other than a little stronger shove against the shoulder, which really amounts to very little when using light field loads, and some minor brass resizing for the handloader, this condition poses no threat to the gun or shooter. And since, in case of the Parker, the cure would be far worse than the disease, it is better to accept it as part of the gun's aging character.

If scrutinized long and hard enough, chinks can be found in any old gun's shining armor. It is not my intent to sully the well-deserved reputation earned by the Parker shotgun by airing a laundry list of its weaknesses. All used guns, regardless of manufacture, have their Achilles' heels. Because my heart goes out to every hunter who wants to shoot his Parker, the troubleshooting done here is to help keep these fine old guns in the uplands.

Parker people are among some of the finest to be found anywhere. Their respect for the guns usually grows to embrace the entire hunting experience. One such man was kind enough to acquaint me with his extensive Parker collection. From his hammer guns on up to a high-grade Remington-Parker, each gun had its own personality. He had shot them all, on waterfowl, trap, skeet, and upland birds. One of his most recent additions was a DHE 12-gauge, two-barreled set. We dismantled the gun, examined it closely, and dropped its hammers on a pair of snap caps for the better part of an evening. The gun was in the 190,000 serial number range and was in overall excellent condition.

One thing that disturbed me about the gun was the way the wood on the splinter forearm seemed to move as the fired gun was opened. My friend explained to me that this wood movement, or creep, was peculiar to ejector guns that had seen a lot of use. Parker ejectors are cocked upon opening, and if the fore-end screws are not kept tight, wood creep will develop. If the problem is allowed to persist, replacement of the fore-end wood may be the only remedy.

Like any very fine machine or mechanism, Parker guns require periodic maintenance. The older the gun, the more tender loving care it should be given. Far too many fine old Parkers are being abused and destroyed by steady diets of magnum and maximum-load shotshells. Such cannon fodder is better left to modern repeaters. If the hunter wants to protect his investment, nothing stronger than field loads should pass through the chambers of his vintage Parker.

Many times the Parker ejector system is blamed for ejection troubles that are really caused by untrained gunsmiths. If, for instance, the chambers are reamed or polished beyond specifications, the fired hulls expand and adhere to the chamber walls, thus preventing the ejectors from doing their job. Because there are so few gunsmiths who possess a thorough working knowledge of Parkers, countless guns continue to be guinea pigs in the hands of ignorance. Incredible as it may sound, more and more Parker barrel ribs, hooks, and lugs must be resoldered each year because some "gunsmith" subjected them to a bath in the hot-bluing tank. Such treatment borders on criminal negligence, especially when the Parker is a family heirloom or a hunter's cherished upland bird gun. Good gunsmiths today are as rare as Invincible Grade Parkers. When you find one, be willing to pay the price of quality workmanship.

Unless specially built for skeet shooting or upland bird hunting, most Parkers, as well as other American classics, have some undesirable traits which must be corrected before they can become true upland performers. Most barrels will be tightly choked and varying in length from thirty to thirty-four inches. The majority will combine full-pistol grips with double triggers and English-style splinter forearms. More often than not, the buttstock will be too short and the drop at the comb and heel too great. To an instinctive-style shooter, such features detract from quick and accurate gun handling and mounting.

If the hunter is willing to alter the original condition of his gun (this always sends Parker collectors into fits of apoplexy), it can be transformed into a more responsive instrument for the uplands.

By replacing the buttstock with one of longer and straighter dimensions, and by modifying the trigger-guard tang to a straight or semi-pistol grip, the gun's handling dynamics will improve substantially. Depending on choice of wood, checkering pattern, and trigger-guard conversion, the entire alteration can be completed by a custom stockmaker and gunsmith in usually less than six months. The cost of such renovation is minimal compared to the time and dollars spent

Parker AAHE Grade 16-gauge. Photo by William W. Headrick, courtesy of Lewis Drake & Associates.

by many hunters who are continually buying, trading, and searching for that "ideal" bird gun. A properly fitted buttstock, one that takes the triggers and forearm into consideration, will cure a covey-full of bird shooting ills. By securing the talents of a competent stocker, the hunter is also assured that the new wood will properly balance out the gun for quick handling afield.

Unless the gun's barrels are uncomfortably long, cutting is not recommended because it can eliminate the gradual forcing cones of the chokes. A better recourse is to have the chokes carefully opened and lapped by a knowledgeable and experienced metalsmith. The paranoia over forcing cones by many bird shooters stems from the belief that shot patterns are improved in direct proportion to the length of the forcing cone, especially when shot columns are "unprotected" by plastic cup wads. Many double-gun hunters, the author included, still prefer to use shotshells made with the old fiber wads. They give a more consistent gas seal under all conditions, and the hunter won't have to wear out his phosphor bronze brush or arm trying to scrub plastic shot-cup fouling from his bores. It also cuts down on the plastic litter found in game fields these days.

Numerous Parkers are found at gun shows and shops with little or no case colors remaining on their receivers or fore-end hardware. This is more often due to the application of a buffing wheel than the aging process. The buffing is bad enough, but what really gives Parker collectors terminal indigestion are receivers and fore-end steel that have been blued. This situation occurs because so few gunsmiths are trained or equipped to properly caseharden gun metal.

Parker's original casehardening process is especially difficult to duplicate; the formula for its brilliance died with the few Parker employees who perfected it. The later Remington-Parkers were color casehardened with the less vibrant cyanide process. When old Parkers are re-casehardened, a slight gapping at the breech often develops around the right barrel. This can be detected by holding the breech area up to a bright light or by inserting a thin piece of typing paper between the right barrel and standing breech. Apparently the pounding the right barrel takes during a lifetime of shooting has a tendency to move it slightly off the face of the action. This condition, combined with a little warping of the frame during the re–casehardening process, can produce a less-than-perfect seal at the breech. Such slight gapping is insignificant and poses no threat to the gun or shooter; it is more of a psychological problem for the purist who insists that his gun be right in every detail.

Another sign of a restored Parker is the metal-to-metal fit around the doll's-head. If there are margins or gaps around any portion of the doll's-head, the gun's jointing has probably been tampered with somewhere along the line. But again, there is really no need for concern. If the strong bolting mechanism on the Parker is functioning properly, the doll's-head fit becomes secondary. It, too, contributed more to psychological well-being and sales appeal than to bank-vault bolting. Proof of the pudding are thousands of Trojan Grade Parkers that are still grinding up cartridges with no doll's-head at all. Proper underbolting, as seen in Winchester's Model 21, eliminates the need for doll's-heads, crossbolts, and other such superfluous bolting devices.

Improper screw alignment is also a good indication that a Parker has been tampered with by unschooled hands. All screw-head slots on the bottom of the receiver and trigger guard should be aligned longitudinally with the barrels and stock. The large hinge-pin screw slot on the right side of the receiver must also be in its proper horizontal alignment. Throughout the gun, all screw-heads must be in their proper vertical or horizontal position. From the highest to the lowest grade, every gun that left Parker was closely examined to ensure that screw slots were in correct alignment. Such attention to detail was characteristic of Parker's entire manufacturing process.

All in all, the Parker shotgun still retains its game gun acceptance among shotgunners because of its hand-built balance and quality workmanship. The higher grades, especially, offer discriminating hunters the wood, checkering, engraving, and other features that foster pride of ownership. For those who prefer to pursue upland birds with a shotgun from the Good Old Days, Parker's "Old Reliable" still lives up to its name.

A. H. FOX

Never built with Damascus barrels, Ansley H. Fox side-by-sides were modern guns wrought from modern steel. Mechanically simple in design, the A. H. Fox is considered by many to be the best boxlock made in America. Since the gun's inception in 1907, coil springs were used throughout, and the quality of its forged steel action and Krupp barrels were touted by many to be second to none. President Teddy Roosevelt extolled the virtues of the Fox shotgun on several occasions. All Foxes were designed with a wear-compensating, rotary-bolting device that protruded from the barrel assembly and locked into a slot milled into the top of the standing breech. Fox's rotary-bolting design, borrowed from L. C. Smith, was so secure that no underbolting was necessary.

Like the Parker, many Foxes were built with full-pistol grips, double triggers, and splinter fore-ends—not exactly an ideal arrangement for the bird shooter, but a straight-grip Fox 16- or 20-gauge with twenty-eight-inch barrels bored improved-cylinder and modified could keep an upland hunter happy for many seasons. Most 12-gauge Fox guns tend to be on the heavy side for upland work, but, depending on the hunter's physique and condition, can be adapted to short morning and afternoon hunts. There is no record of any factory-built .410, 28, or 10-gauge Fox shotguns. Just over 200,000 Foxes were produced during its forty-four-year history.

The Fox was fitted with non-rebounding hammers, which some have claimed makes it more difficult to open after firing, the firing pins apparently dragging across the spent primers. Fox countered this claim by stating that the lock time (firing speed) of its guns was faster than its competition's rebounding hammer models. Whatever the case, the Fox is a proven performer and a beautiful work of art in its higher grades. Its options included ejectors, single selective trigger, beavertail forearm, and many others.

During the first half of this century, waterfowlers such as Nash Buckingham were very fond of A. H. Fox magnum shotguns. Fox doubles were given a rigorous test in cold, damp duck blinds across the country. Any gun design that can withstand the heavy loads and inclement weather of wildfowling will have little trouble giving generations of service in the uplands. There is something very comforting about the sound of a Fox action camming shut. The rotary bolt locks with decided authority, giving the hunter a feeling of security and peace of mind as he steps into the field.

Perhaps the reason more gunsmiths prefer the Fox action to other designs is because of its simplicity and ease of maintenance. As such, the Fox owner will probably have less difficulty finding a gunsmith competent enough to repair his shotgun. However, experience is still the best teacher, and it would behoove the serious hunter to have his double serviced by someone well schooled in the care and feeding of a Fox.

L. C. SMITH

America's most revered sidelock, the L. C. Smith, has become a legend among knowledgeable hunters and collectors. Its graceful lines are as pleasing to the eye in the unadorned lower grades as they are in the breathtakingly engraved and gold-inlayed higher grades. The L. C. Smith was made with a tapered rotary-bolting mechanism that provided a very solid lockup. Its simple sidelocks deliver crisp trigger-pulls, and the gun was offered in a variety of gauges and weights. A lightweight L. C. Smith in 12-, 16-, or 20-gauge is a delight to carry in the uplands.

America's predilection for pistol grips and double triggers combined with English-style fore-ends also impacted the handling dynamics of the L. C. Smith. But a lightweight, straight-grip Smith is a vision any bird hunter would enjoy shooting. From field grade to Deluxe, every Smith reflected a standard of quality that guaranteed it a position of honor among America's best. As on most production guns, the wood and checkering found on the lower grades was often plain and simple. A field-grade Smith, though lacking any engraving, becomes a thing of beauty when correctly restocked in full fancy walnut.

Whether low or high grade, most used L. C. Smiths are prone to wood cracks around the lockplates. The cracking results from a hasty job of inletting the wood to the back face of the action. Unless a precise inletting job is achieved here, the stress of recoil will be conducted through the lockplates, causing hairline wood cracks to develop around the lock work. These cracks are seldom serious enough to jeopardize the functional integrity of the gun, but they do detract from its well-earned reputation of quality and workmanship. In some instances, especially on the wood at the bottom of the sideplates along the triggers, the cracking may become severe and require repair. This condition is further aggravated by extremes in temperature and humidity during storage of the gun. L. C. Smiths that have been restocked by a skilled stocker (with air-dried walnut containing the proper moisture content) are less likely to develop cracks. Many of these headaches can be avoided by keeping action screws snug.

The cost of restocking an otherwise mechanically sound "Sweet Elsie" is relatively small when compared to the many seasons of shooting pleasure it will give the upland hunter.

During the height of the Machine Age, when America was flexing its industrial might around the world, gunmakers such as Baker, Lefever, Ithaca, Remington, and others combined modern production methods with meticulous hand-craftsmanship to create an American Golden Age in sporting arms design and development. Along with Parker, Fox, and L. C. Smith, they created a legacy in a few short decades that still causes deep pangs of nostalgia among dedicated double-gun enthusiasts today. Anyone possessing a higher grade American "best" has little to envy from other game gun makers around the world, past or present.

A latecomer to America's classic double-gun parade was the Winchester Model 21. Though somewhat on the heavy side for rigorous upland work, the Model 21's entry during the Depression years of the 1930s must have imbued it with a certain strength of character, because out of all the others, it was the last of America's Golden Age doubles to venture into the last half of the twentieth century.

Photo courtesy John Hanusin

7

THE MODERN CLASSICS

THE COMMON MARKET MAY CONTROL the financial purse of Europe, but cultural centers such as St. Etienne, France; Liège, Belgium; Ferlach, Austria; Suhl, Germany; Eibar, Spain; and Brescia, Italy, are known worldwide for the fine sporting arms they produce.

European gunmakers, though often emulating English game gun designs, have crafted fine double shotguns for centuries. One need only inspect a French Granger, a Spanish Garbi, or Italian Piotti to realize that hunters around the world still demand the best game guns skilled hands can create.

Through selected importers and traveling sportsmen, game guns from Europe and elsewhere are meeting with eager acceptance among discriminating shotgunners in the United States. And well they should; Old World craftsmanship is still motivated more by pride and quality than by bottom-line profits.

The same wars that often fueled firearms development across Europe also took their toll on the master craftsmen who built fine sporting arms. The manpower drain caused by two world wars all but broke the back of the master/apprentice system that had existed for generations in Europe. Without the old masters to pass along the tricks of the trade, the quality of Europe's gunmaking after the great wars steadily declined. The same fate was visited on the British Isles. This circumstance, coupled with the mass production of machine-made pumps and autoloading shotguns, accelerated the decline of the classic double gun. However, in Europe, as in England, tradition has a tenacity for life seldom understood by pragmatic Americans.

Double guns are still the choice of knowledgeable European sportsmen, and a new generation of gunmakers is catering to the demand with shotguns reminiscent of the great guns built by their grandfathers.

Though England may lay claim to its modern design and development, the game gun was really born in France. Nearly 300 years ago, the French introduced their sport of wingshooting to the British. Many of the early pinfire and breechloading shotgun designs were pioneered by such Frenchmen as Lefaucheaux, Boutet, and Devimers. As such, perhaps it is fitting that France be the first country discussed in the development of the European game gun.

FRANCE

Unfortunately, France today is not the sporting-arms center it once was. Though a few of its gunmakers still make side-by-sides that can compete with the best of them, France no longer captures the sportsman's imagination or money the way it did in years past. The French lost an incredible number of good men during the world wars, which no doubt cut into their supply of craftsmen and into their market.

But the noble French still have a few gunmakers who can turn heads with their workmanship. Notable among them is Georges Granger whose sidelock doubles rival England's best. The French walnut is of the highest quality, and it is precisely inletted to finely finished and engraved gun steel. For decades, French walnut has been the choice of all best-gun makers, and Granger uses some of the finest. Production of Granger's side-by-sides, because of their extensive hand-craftsmanship, is limited to only a few dozen each year. As one can imagine, the cost of these beautiful guns is as high as the quality, but not unreachable by well-heeled sportsmen.

The Darne, with its novel sliding breech, is still sought by upland gunners who are looking for a lightweight game gun. In its higher grades, the Darne is ornately engraved and handsomely checkered. The Darne's sliding breech action is very strong and firmly locks cartridge heads into their chambers; few head-spacing problems are ever encountered when buying a used Darne. Though a simple sliding breech, the mechanism still selectively ejects spent hulls while partially extracting unfired cartridges. Hunters who handload their shells will find the Darne action most accommodating, as it can lever the most stubborn of cartridges into and out of its chambers.

The Darne is a wonderfully balanced, lightweight game gun of exceptional value and quality. In recent years, the company has teetered on the brink of extinction, but its guns are still being crafted by proud Frenchmen over the factory's same earthen floors trod by past generations of St. Etienne craftsmen.

Another French gunmaker currently importing double guns into the U.S. is Vouzlaud. Nearly a hundred years old, Vouzlaud produces a very reasonably priced boxlock game gun that is beautifully fitted and finished. The gun can also be ordered with dummy sideplates for added ornamentation. Only the finest steel forgings are used in construction of its barrels and receiver. The chopper lump barrels close on an Anson-and-Deeley-style action similar to that of the Webley & Scott of England—a portion of the forward barrel lug extending through the bottom plate of the action. A third grip is neatly tucked between the ejectors for added strength. Depending on shooter preference, Vouzlaud receivers are either casehardened or finished in satin gray.

Whether scroll or game scene, the engraving is well executed, tastefully enhancing the lines of the gun. Perhaps one of the most stunning aspects of each Vouzlaud is the quality of the wood. Taken from the Perigord region of France, the highly figured walnut ranges in color from light to reddish to dark, and is cleanly checkered at about thirty lines to the inch. Because the guns are entirely handcrafted, their production is limited. Special-order guns require three to eight months for delivery.

During a recent visit to a gun shop, I shouldered a thirty-year-old French boxlock double that took my breath away. The gun was in almost mint condition and fit me like a comfortable loafer. Built for a prestigious department store in Paris by a St. Etienne gunmaker (VL&A in America also imported private-label shotguns by Old World gunmakers), the 12-gauge game gun whispered sweet nothings in my ear every time I brought it to my shoulder. Its snappy ejectors kicked empty hulls halfway across the store, and its wood-to-metal and metal-to-metal fit was superb. As I write this, I am still trying to figure out a way to raid the domestic treasury and smuggle that lovely gun into my house.

My wife, a beautiful woman of French ancestry though she may be, would guillotine me in a second if she knew I was scheming to bring another shotgun home, French or otherwise. I sometimes believe she would be more apt to forgive my indiscretion with another woman than see me shut away in my den playing with another shotgun. Ahh! But in France such triangles are the spice of life. And the day true gun lovers cease to lust after comely, hand-built side-by-sides will be a sad one for the French or anyone else with passionate blood in their veins.

BELGIUM

The gunmakers of Liège, Belgium have exported their beautifully built barrels to England and other countries for hundreds of years. During the mid-nineteenth century, these crafty gunmakers were also responsible for merchandising the name "Damascus" as a trade name for their brand of twist steel barrels. The Belgians were keenly aware of the worldwide reputation that fine cutlery from Damascus had created during that era and capitalized on it in their barrelmaking. As a result, the name Damascus has become generic for the old twist steel barrelmaking process.

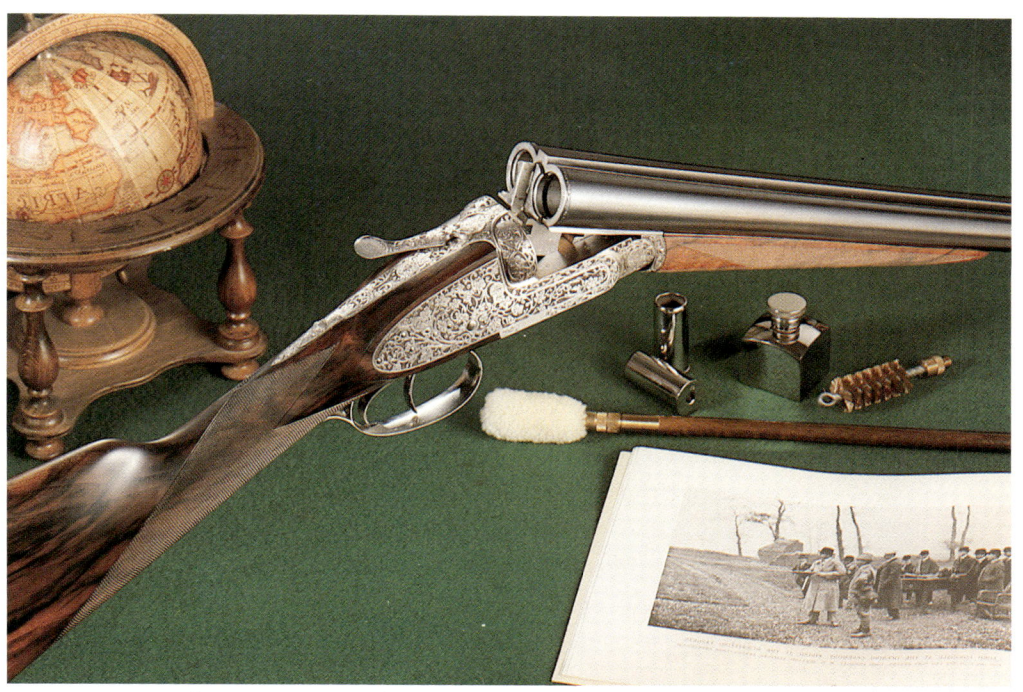

European gunmakers continue to build state-of-the-art game guns that are beautiful and shootable. Photo courtesy of William Larkin Moore & Co.

As quality conscious as they are shrewd, the better gunmakers in Liège are producing game guns today that require little fanfare or introduction. Francotte is one such gunmaker. Whether boxlock or sidelock, every Francotte is a work of art that performs in the field. For years, Ambercrombie & Fitch made these high-quality guns available to its customers. Considering their hand-built virtues, the guns are not outrageously priced and can be had for less than the cost of most sub-compact cars. And unlike the cars, a Francotte will not depreciate in value as the years slip away.

Francotte's gold inlay work is also unusually well executed. Setters look like setters, grouse look like grouse, and both look lifelike posed on a Francotte sideplate. All gauges are properly proportioned, with barrels and stock gracefully contoured. Every Francotte is built to last a lifetime and then some. Knowledgeable shotgunners respect the name as much as they admire the handling and shooting qualities of this prestigious Belgian gunmaker.

A truly classic line of boxlocks and sidelocks to suit the double-gun connoisseur is offered by Lebeau-Courally. The quality of these fine doubles is second to none. Patterned after proven Purdey and Holland & Holland designs, Lebeau-Courally's prices parallel those of the English gunmakers they emulate. Such guns are costly in every country that builds game guns. The time and handcraftsmanship involved is tremendous, but so is the pleasure of owning the best.

Another firm which has benefitted from its association with Belgian gunmakers is Browning Arms. Browning over-unders made by Fabrique Nationale in Belgium continue to command good prices on the used gun market. The same holds true for Browning's Belgian-made A5 autoloader. The high-grade over-unders made in Liège for Browning reflect the highest standard of handcraftsmanship. Though they are not side-by-side game guns, they are an indication of the kind of work the Belgians are producing.

Years ago, I paid gunsmiths in vain to tighten the breech of a sweet-handling boxlock made by an unknown gunmaker. The gun's origin was identified by two words on the right barrel—"Liège, Belgium." Along with its Anson and Deeley action, it had a Greener-style crossbolt that couldn't be tightened for love nor money. The rattle at the breech became annoying if not dangerous. I traded the gun for a new, but cheap, Spanish double, which is another story.

Like many gunmaking centers, Liège has produced its share of shoddy craftsmanship to snare the unwary. But to bad-mouth all Belgian gunmakers for the sins of a few is less than fair; the better Belgian gunmakers can compete with master craftsmen from any country or continent.

If you should ever run across a Neuman double and are reluctant to buy it because of its Belgian moniker, drop me a note, I'll find a good home for it. After all, it is a rather plain little boxlock. That its streamlined profile can be easily trained to hunt American grouse, woodcock, and quail is no doubt of little significance to those who are hung up on names.

Unexcelled craftsmanship is reflected in this Belgian-made Lebeau-Courally 20-gauge. Photo courtesy of William Larkin Moore & Co.

SPAIN

During my initiation years, I bought a cheap Spanish double 20-gauge that cracked like a rifle and kicked like a mule. Had I let that gun serve as an example of Spanish gunmaking skills, I would have been denied the pleasure of owning a truly fine Spanish shotgun.

Taking advantage of cheap labor and a willing market, early importers of Spanish doubles lined their silk purses with profits from the sow's ears they passed off as good double guns. Not only did they do their customers a disservice, but they also helped to instill mistrust in double guns carrying Spanish labels.

While many gun writers and shotgunners were ignoring Spanish offerings, a number of gunmakers in Eibar quietly continued to build some of the finest firearms available. On *la perdiz roja* (red-legged partridge) hunting excursions over the Castillian countryside and at prestigious live-pigeon shoots across Spain, shotgunners from America, England, and Europe began to take notice of the high-grade Spanish doubles being used with success in the gaming fields.

Eventually, a new breed of importers began to show interest in the Spanish gun trade. Bringing with them rigid manufacturing guidelines to complement the high-quality standards and rigorous government proofing of Spanish guns, these importers began to showcase double guns of great quality for a reasonable price. They also found that pride in craftsmanship was still alive and growing stronger among Spanish artisans.

If any gunmakers have patterned themselves after the old English gun trade, the better gun houses in Eibar, Spain, most certainly have. The smaller firms, especially, employ master and apprentice artisans who build guns from the ground up with simple hand tools.

Perhaps the largest gunmaker in Spain, if not in Europe, is AyA. Using modern machinery wherever possible, this firm produces a wide variety of sidelock and boxlock game guns, many of which are exported to England and the United States. In the higher grades, the guns are almost carbon copies of proven English game gun designs, proportions, and weights, and AyA backs each of its guns with a strong guarantee on parts and workmanship.

The firm uses straight-grained Spanish walnut of rather plain figure, but higher-grade wood can be ordered. Having never put hundreds of cases of cartridges through an AyA side-by-side, I cannot vouch for their longevity or ability to withstand the pounding of a competitive clay-bird shooter. However, I have yet to hear any complaints from hunters about these guns shooting loose in the field.

The serious upland bird hunter who is searching for a superior game gun need look no further than the high-grade offerings

The Modern Classics

In keeping with past Renaissance masters, Italian gunmakers are building double guns of breathtaking beauty, as evidenced by the Rizzini 20-gauge sidelock. Photo courtesy of William Larkin Moore & Co.

built by a talented guild of artisans known as Armas Garbi. Garbi collected some of Eibar's finest gunmakers with the goal of producing the best double guns in Spain. Many agree that he has already succeeded. Again, his shotguns follow traditional English patterns, particularly Holland & Holland, and are embellished with fine rose-and-scroll and game-scene engravings. The sportsman can also special order guns with gold inlay work. England has proved to be a

Garbi Model 103A Special. Photo courtesy of William Larkin Moore & Co.

most willing recipient of Garbi guns, which should tell you something. Eager to please such a discriminating market, Garbi continues to upgrade and refine his production methods. The fit, feel, and handling qualities of a high-grade Garbi sidelock make it a very good investment for the upland hunter who can't afford an English "best" but is not willing to settle for less.

I still lament the loss of a 16-gauge Garbi sidelock that I let a hunting partner talk me out of. It had an exceptional piece of wood that was meticulously inletted to the locks and action. My friend moved away, and that Garbi was one of the first things he packed up before he left—he knew I'd drop by to try to talk him into selling it back.

With the guidance and advice of Orvis gunsmiths, Arrieta is building sidelock game guns for export to the United States that are exceptional values. Their barrels are smoothly struck, their checkering is precise, and their metal casehardening and tempering is

Piotti's Model King Extra is a shining example of Italian artistry.

Garbi Models (top to bottom) 101 CC, 100, and 100 CF. Photo courtesy of William Larkin Moore & Co.

excellent. Anyone who has attended one of Orvis' shooting schools will no doubt see more than a few of these guns in service. Though showing external wear, the hand-polished sidelocks are still grinding up hunters' clays without fail. All are custom-order guns offering the shooter a complete list of options, including individually tailored gunstocks.

  I shot a round of skeet with an Orvis gun that had been fitted for a right-handed shooter. Shooting international style (gun down until the target appears), I broke eighteen birds from the left shoulder. The gun pointed quickly and smoothly. I was also impressed by its precise wood-to-metal fit. It, like other better Spanish side-by-sides, offers the dollar-conscious bird hunter a game gun that will last a lifetime.

  Game gun making is reaching its golden age in Spain with firms such as Arizabalaga, Arrieta, and Garbi all contributing to the renaissance. The game gun enthusiast whose budget is beleaguered by the high cost of just staying alive these days would do well to check out what Spain has to offer. When compared with England's best, they will no doubt present a few shortcomings to the purist, but to the upland hunter who still seeks pride in ownership, a good Spanish double will provide years of shooting pleasure.

GERMANY

With automobiles like the Mercedes and the Porsche to their credit, German craftsmen are renowned for their engineering and metallurgical prowess. Their obsession with precision workmanship manifests itself in their sporting arms as well. Anyone who has an affinity for hairline tolerances and mechanisms that function like a jeweled Swiss watch will appreciate German-built shotguns.

In general, German side-by-side shotguns do not honor the classic lines or embellishment of English or other European game guns. German doubles are multi-purpose guns that are used to hunt running game as well as game birds. Often found with full-pistol grips and considerable drop at the comb and heel, German gunstocks are reminiscent of some of America's early scatterguns. *Jaegers* (German hunters) also like cheekpieces, sling swivels, horn inlays, and heavy carving on their stocks.

Engraving on German game guns is also executed in bold fashion with oak leaves carved around the fences, jumping hares, baying hounds, and leaping stags chiseled onto the receiver, with bas-relief scrollwork accentuating the game scenes. The Germans are not modest about their affection towards hunting, eagerly chiseling it into wood and steel. You either like their bold style or you don't. However, some of the side-by-sides made by Simpson of Suhl, Germany, were finished in fine scroll engraving for export to England and to other countries. The German craftsman is capable of rendering almost any style of firearms engraving and stock finishing. Those owning a Prussian Charles Daly can witness the refined elegance the German master gunmaker can build into a double.

Merkel is a well-known firm whose side-by-side shotguns reflect proper game gun breeding. The company builds boxlock and sidelock guns that are as handsome as they are quick handling. Pre-war

Merkels are of exceptionally fine quality and are aggressively sought by collectors. The Germans, too, suffered the ravages of war that crippled their craftsmanship for some time. Today's Merkels still provide a standard of metalwork and wood-to-metal fit that will bring a gleam to the eye of most discriminating bird hunters.

Probably known more for their drillings (combination shotguns and rifles), J. P. Sauer & Sons also builds high-quality guns that are suitable for the uplands. Like Greener, the Germans are still fond of crossbolts, and many of Sauer's side-by-sides carry this feature. Because of their emphasis on action strength and heavy metalwork, Sauer 12-gauge doubles can weigh over seven pounds. Sixteen-gauge Sauers, on the other hand, are a bird of a different feather and will perform well in the uplands. Fortunately, the 16-gauge is still embraced in Germany and other European countries for upland hunting purposes.

Competition in today's double-gun market has pretty well weeded out the poor-quality doubles that gave German gunmakers a sullied reputation half a century ago. It seems every gunmaking country has had its turn in the thresher, the chaff getting sorted from the grain. German gunmakers can hold their heads high, as can anyone who owns a well-made German double gun.

AUSTRIA

The Austrians produce some of the world's best gunsmiths, as well as a select number of side-by-side shotguns. Similar to the Germans in their quest for hairline tolerances, Austrian gunmakers such as Franz Sodia build doubles that last generations.

Ferlach is the hub of Austria's gun trade, producing both high-quality double shotguns and rifles. Whether Germanic or English in style, Austrian game guns are jewels of old-fashioned craftsmanship. The world's gun trade is well aware of Austria's ability to fashion quality gun steel, and Austrian barrels and actions are exported to prestigious gunmaking houses in other European countries as well as Great Britain. Because most gunmaking in Austria is on a custom-order basis, output is limited. Austrians make few standard-grade shotguns.

The classic Piotti gun, simply adorned, still catches the eye with its symmetry.

Austrian gunmaking today is structured similar to the vintage English gun trade in structure, forming an interdependent cooperative of barrelmakers, actioners, stockers, lockmakers, and other suppliers. Their combined talents produce some of the finest sporting arms available. Austrians are as proud to build such high-quality game guns as most hunters are to own them.

ITALY

The Italians have a passion for beauty that permeates their entire lifestyle. From racing cars to film stars, Italians love a classic form that functions with elegance. Their sporting shotguns are an extension of their perennial quest for beauty.

Brescia, Italy, is to game guns what Paris is to art. Following in the footsteps of Leonardo DaVinci and Michelangelo, Italian gunmakers are creating works in metal and wood that could easily grace the halls of a neo-classical art museum. They have carried the tradition of game gun making to its pinnacle of development. Though patterned after English designs, Italian game guns combine the best of modern technology with Old World craftsmanship. The end product embodies the best of both worlds, offering shotgunners game guns that are as pleasing to the senses as they are a joy to carry afield.

As one would expect, the price of an Italian "best" can make even the most prosperous among us suck a little wind, but with some

Italian-made FERLIB reflects excellent fit and finish.

luck and creative financing, it is possible to pick up a used double without incurring the wrath of one's creditors or spouse.

Fabbri, Famars, Rizzini, Perazzi, Piotti, Beretta, Bernardelli, and FERLIB will build sidelock and boxlock game guns that are above reproach, so much so, in fact, that it is often difficult for the hunter to subject them to the molestations of hill and dale. But the real beauty of a game gun is its ability to withstand hard use. High-grade Italian guns are as tough as they are beautiful.

Italian gunmakers, by and large, are meticulous about the fit and finish of their guns. Metal appears to melt into metal at the breech, barrel flats, and hinge. Buttstock and forearm walnut grafts itself around gun steel in perfect harmony. Engraving ranges from the ornate to the sublime. Bulino game scenes exhibit such photographic detail that it is difficult to believe the engraving was accomplished with a simple hand tool; Fabbri and Famars are particularly renowned for their bulino engraved masterpieces. Italian engravers can also produce delicate English rose-and-scroll patterns to completely cover a sidelock or enhance the design of a game scene. Anyone who inspects a Piotti will appreciate the fine scroll in the Model King No. 1 and the Renaissance style, deep-relief scroll on the Model Lunik.

Small-bore game guns seem to have captured the fancy of many sportsmen and collectors in the United States; double guns in .410 and 28-gauge are bringing premium prices. I must admit that a small-bore Rizzini or FERLIB is a precious gem of workmanship which would make any woodcock hunter happy.

Beretta, one of the oldest gunmaking families in Italy, produces doubles around a monoblock breech and barrel assembly. The breech is forged as a unit and milled to receive the barrels, not unlike the barrel sleeving process developed by the English to convert the old Damascus-barrel guns. A Beretta SO-7 sidelock is a beautifully built game gun.

For those desiring a moderately priced double gun of very good quality, Bernardelli offers a classic line of boxlock and sidelock game guns. For years, Stoeger imported Bernardelli doubles built along English lines, which represented a very good value for the dollar. Occasionally, one will turn up at a gun show or sporting goods store where the sellers are often as much at a loss to determine an asking price as the buyers are to recognize a good investment.

Perazzi is a name with which trapshooters readily identify. The sleek, businesslike over-unders built by this high-quality gunmaker are world renowned for their consistency in grinding up clay birds. However, this well-earned reputation often overshadows the very fine side-by-side doubles Perazzi builds. There are more than a few live-pigeon shooters who would rather be caught naked at a shoot than be without their Perazzi. A few years back, I was privileged to shoot a matched pair of highly engraved, gold-inlayed Perazzi sidelocks that made me think twice about why I got married and up to my ears in debt.

The Italians have accepted England's flickering gunmaking torch and are building game guns that will keep the flame burning brightly for years to come. Such quality workmanship is a tribute to every man whose heart still burns with a passion to hunt.

SCOTLAND

Known more for their parsimonious nature than as a gunmaking people, the Scots can take great pride in a member of their clan who created one of the most revered and envied game-gun action designs in the world—the Dickson "Round Action." John Dickson of Edinburgh, Scotland, began a legacy in gunmaking during the nineteenth century that lives on today. His round action, in both boxlock and sidelock ejector guns, found immediate favor with hunters who liked the way it snuggled comfortably in the crook of the arm or over the shoulder. The graceful action also allows the exceptionally fine scrollwork found on all Dickson shotguns to flow uninterrupted around the action body.

As durable as they are attractive, Dickson doubles are an artist's blend of beautifully casehardened metal, sharply defined checkering, and highly figured walnut. They are true hunting guns.

Dickson side-by-side doubles function as smoothly mechanically as they do in the field. But it was really a triple-barrelled gun of older vintage that gave me a clearer insight into the gunmaking genius of John Dickson. The straight-gripped gun was an elegant Damascus side-by-side 16-gauge. It was beautifully balanced and not the least bit cumbersome to handle. The side lever opened barrels that fit firmly to the breech, and its selective ejectors worked flawlessly. Its twin triggers were crisp and sure, the front trigger firing the right and center barrels and the rear trigger discharging the left barrel. The engraving and woodwork were of such fine quality that even those unfamiliar with gunmaking were impressed by it. The gun, in excellent condition in spite of its age, had been donated to Ducks

Unlimited to help raise funds for that organization's conservation efforts. It was auctioned to a Dickson collector who now owns what has to be considered one of the rarest works of art in metal and wood ever to leave a gunmaker's bench.

Other Scottish gunmakers, such as Mortimer & Son, Forbes, and Henry have all left their stamp of quality on the gun trade. Their guns, like the country's fine split-cane rods, were never produced in any great quantities because they were patiently and painstakingly built one at a time. And though England may take credit as the cradle of modern game gun design, old John Dickson lit a fire under the gun trade that still burns brightly today.

JAPAN

Often maligned for the cheap and trashy trinkets it produced for the world market during the 1940s and '50s, Japan today challenges the free world with electronics gear, automobiles, and sporting arms of very high quality. No longer does "Made in Japan" carry with it the stigma of inferior craftsmanship it once did.

As labor costs escalated during the 1960s, some of America's firearms manufacturers turned to Japan to produce quality shotguns at a competitive price. Charles Daly (not to be confused with the Prussian Daly) introduced a line of side-by-side and over-under doubles by B. C. Miroku of Japan for import to the United States. Ithaca, Winchester, and Browning soon followed, and the quality of Japanese gunmaking began to increase in proportion to the competition.

I put a Charles Daly Model 500 side-by-side (which at the time was sold with a lifetime guarantee) through its paces and found it to be a solid performer. The gun was patterned similarly to the Winchester Model 21, sporting a full-pistol grip, streamlined beavertail, and a vent rib. Unlike the 21, the gun was equipped with double triggers and extractors. Its metal-to-metal fit was precise and remained that way after several seasons of heavy use. The only fault I could find with the gun was its inconsistent wood-to-metal fit and crude checkering, but many Chinese ringnecks fell in front of its Japanese muzzles.

Regretfully, in my youthful haste to impress some forgotten but shapely woman, I sold the gun and squandered the money on her vanity. At least I knew from which direction the gun would shoot. The lady spun me around a few times, then lowered the boom. I miss that Japanese Daly and am certain it is serving its new owner as faithfully as it did me. Wish I could say the same for the lady.

Many authorities still consider the chrome-lined bores of SKB's side-by-side to be one of the best production guns ever made. Introduced by Ithaca during the mid-1960s, the SKB Models 100, 200, and 280 offered upland hunters mechanically sound doubles at a reasonable price. The quality and finish of the wood was often disappointing in the earlier models, but improved somewhat after SKB began to offer the guns direct, without the Ithaca affiliation. I have handled a few custom-stocked SKB side-by-sides that left little to be desired in terms of handling and pointability. These boxlock doubles are going to be around for quite some time, offering further evidence that the Japanese can make guns of good reputation.

Browning is a name synonymous with quality, and the double guns it is making in Japan are in keeping with the name. Its English-style boxlock and sidelock side-by-sides offer upland hunters classic double guns that are handsome and durable.

The Browning BSS Sporter was built upon the tried-and-true Anson and Deeley action, while their sidelock followed the traditional Holland & Holland design. The metalwork and engraving on the sidelock is almost flawless, and the wood-to-metal fit is quite good. The walnut found on both models, though straight grained, is rather bland. The quality of checkering is better than average for Japanese-built guns, but could still use improvement. Both guns are finished in typical Browning fashion with lustrous bluing and well-polished metal. Oil-finished stocks also add a traditional touch. For the budget-conscious sportsman interested in a well-balanced, dependable game gun, the Browning boxlock Sporter or sidelock will give him his money's worth.

Winchester was one of America's first major firearms manufacturers to contract with the Japanese to build its extensive line of over-unders. The guns were introduced in the early 1960s primarily to compete with Browning's higher priced, Liège-built over-under. Winchester's only side-by-side offering was the Model 23. A rugged boxlock, the Model 23 was also offered in English game gun style with game-scene engraving, a straight grip, and thinner beavertail forend. The walnut on many of the Model 23s displays more figure than most other double guns from Japan. Checkering patterns are well designed, but the quality of checkering is still not in keeping with the gun's overall fit and finish. The Model 23 lightweight is a good production-grade game gun and will still provide many seasons of enjoyment for the upland hunter.

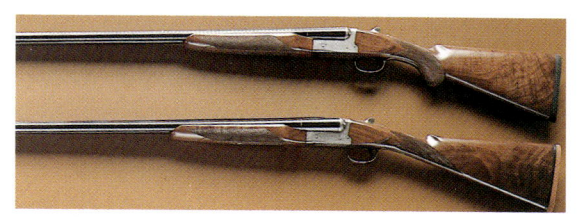

Winchester Model 23 side-by-side offers considerable value for the dollar.

Winchester also produced a reproduction of America's classic Parker. In almost every detail, the gun is a duplicate of an original 20-gauge Parker DHE grade. The guns I have inspected had excellent metal-to-metal tolerances and the wood was mated nicely to the metal on the buttstock and forearm. They were offered in both pistol- and straight-grip models with standard drop dimensions at the comb and heel. The guns handle well, but I was disappointed by the quality of the casehardening and checkering. The top rib also seemed a bit wider than the old Parkers, and the buttstock was proportioned larger than original 20-gauge Parkers I have shot. Whether or not the parts on the reproduction Parkers are truly interchangeable with original guns, as claimed, remains to be seen. Even though all the parts on original Parkers were machined, a great deal of hand-fitting went into each gun. As such, no two guns leaving the Parker factory were identical in every aspect.

But what is really compelling about this Parker reproduction by Winchester is the sporting tradition that spawned it. With original Parkers becoming more and more scarce each day, it is only logical that some enterprising outfit would seek to capitalize on the gun's popularity among upland hunters. I would not hesitate to hunt with

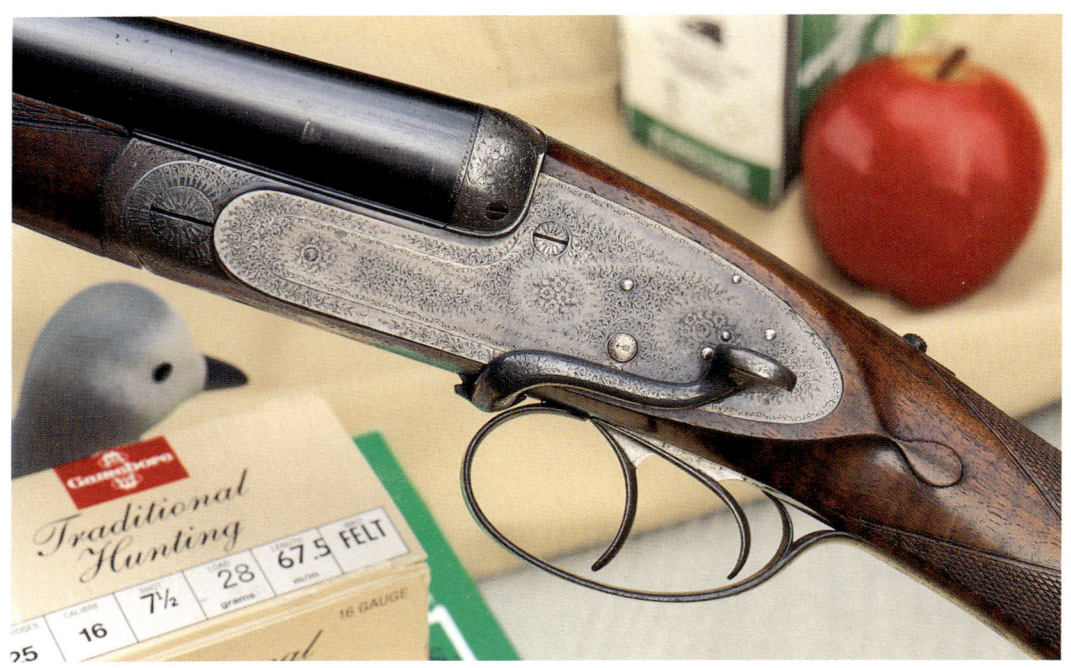

Purdey 16-gauge. Photo by William W. Headrick, courtesy of Lewis Drake & Associates.

this gun. As years go by, and depending on its popularity, the reproduction Parker will continue to hold its value. If it helps to keep alive the sporting legacy alive that gave life to Parker's original shotguns, then it will have served its purpose well.

Japanese double guns will no doubt continue to have an impact on the world market. If their quality continues to improve, more and more upland hunters will no longer let "Made in Japan" stand in the way of owning a gun that will give them many seasons of enjoyment.

ENGLAND

The handwriting is on the wall: The gun trade in grand old England is hurting from too little demand and too much competition. Although some master craftsmen may lament the fact, England is no longer the mecca for game guns it once was prior to the last great war. Pride and tradition, though, will enable such esteemed makers as Purdey, Holland & Holland, Boss, and Westley Richards to continue to build the small quantity of guns that trickle through their doors each year.

As further proof of a faltering trade, even some of England's most prestigious gun houses have been forced to turn to foreign shores for barrels, actions, and other gun parts. It is a sad commentary on a trade that once set a standard of firearms excellence around the world. The British will continue to make a few good guns, but unless a massive transfusion of enthusiasm and dollars is pumped into the system soon, England's once dynamic gun trade will continue to wither away, and with it will go the generations of gunmaking experience and expertise that elevated England's game guns to best in the world.

I fervently hope British gunmakers can hold on long enough to catch the pendulum that will inevitably swing their way as a sleeping America rediscovers the joy of handling a truly hand-built English game gun. As years go by, more and more American hunters will demand high-quality side-by-sides. If the trade is strong enough to survive, the English gunmakers will be capable of meeting that demand (W. & C. Scott is a good example of a firm that is combining quantity and quality to produce competitively priced double guns). If not, those privileged enough to own an English "best" will possess a treasure that will grow in value with each passing generation, and those privileged enough to hunt upland birds with an English game gun will experience an indescribable joy few other guns will ever duplicate. At one time, they were truly the best guns money could buy and are still very worthwhile investments.

Purdey 20-gauge over-under. Photo by William W. Headrick, courtesy of Lewis Drake & Associates.

8

Over-Under

During the latter half of the nineteenth century, when English gunmakers were rushing headlong to adapt shotgun form and function to "shooting flying," numerous barrel configurations, stock designs, and action types reverberated through the thriving gun trade in London and Birmingham. Two-barrel, three-barrel and four-barrel guns, with interesting actions and clever lock and trigger arrangements, briefly captivated the sporting fraternity.

Precursor to the modern English side-by-side game gun, the over-under double was actually the first practical barrel arrangement adopted and discarded by British gunmakers. The modern double gun evolved out of a demand for more firepower by French and English fowlers who pursued the exciting new sport of shooting wild game birds on the wing. Over-unders were the obvious solution to the limitations imposed by early nineteenth century ignition systems which, out of necessity, favored the vertical arrangement. As soon as lock mechanisms were developed to effectively tap flint and percussion, the side-by-side game gun swept the gunmaking field. When the over-under resurfaced again early in the twentieth century, modern metallurgy and centerfire shotshells, along with some innovative engineering by Messieurs Woodward and Boss of England, sowed the seeds for a double-gun renaissance which ultimately produced the bountiful harvest of European and American over-unders on the market today.

The thoroughly British moniker "under-and-over," in the halcyon days when the double trigger reigned supreme, referred to the firing sequence of the barrels—the front trigger discharging the under barrel and the back trigger torching the normally tighter-choked over barrel. Some convention-bound English gunmakers still use the archaic term when referencing the over-under. Tradition often dies hard on the lionized isles. America's legions of free-thinking gun scribes have since taken liberty to pen a bevy of double-barrel descriptions ranging from "stack barrels" and "vertical tubes" to "super-imposed," and the more generic "over-under."

With the advent of breechloading shotguns, game gun makers faced the challenge of building double guns that were well balanced, dependable, and long lived. The ever present nemesis of a prematurely loose, gaping breech spawned a plethora of bolting devices, from the ridiculous and gauche to the sublime and refined. Because side-by-sides were somewhat easier to bolt and balance, they quickly dominated the shooting field. However, the allure of vertically positioned barrels did not deter all Anglo-Saxon gunnies from striving to conquer the twin dragons of over-under bolting and balance. Some early attempts proved to be needlessly complicated and ponderous. By their very nature, over-unders require a deeper frame, greater opening arc and fuller fore-end. All of these elements, if not properly balanced in weight and proportion, serve to depress the seamless handling characteristics demanded by instinctive game shooting.

As with most things pertaining to modern shotgunnery and the high seas, Brittania established the high-water mark for over-under design and performance. In their determined efforts to keep the center of balance low and between the hands, English gunmakers

Over-Under

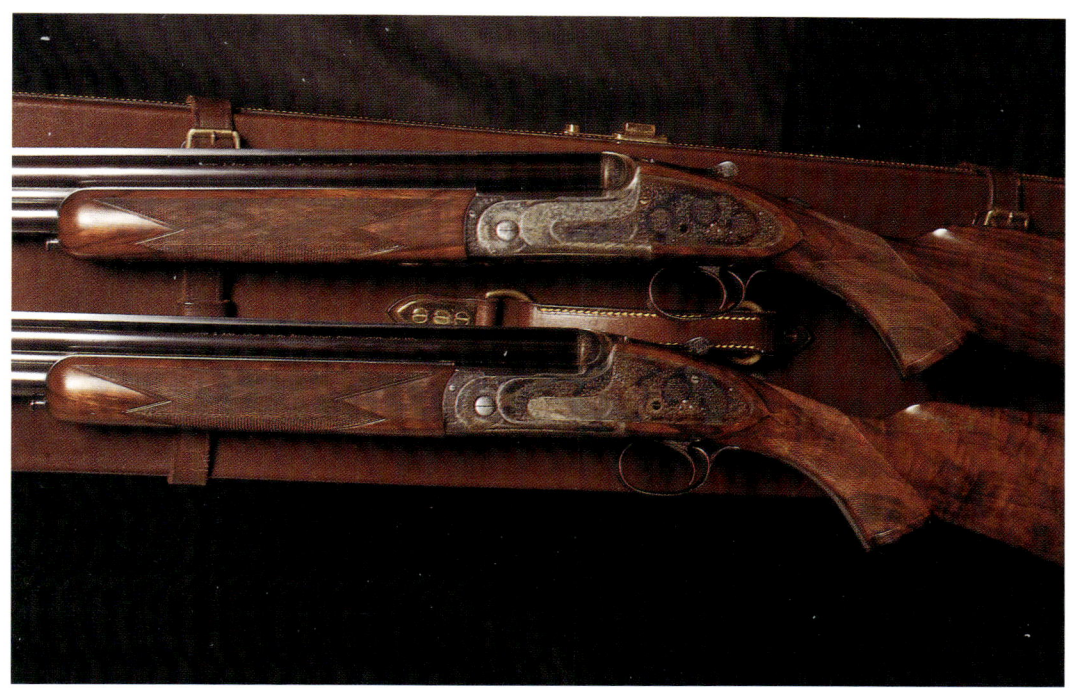

A matched pair of Purdey over-unders. Photo courtesy of John Corry

created over-under bolting systems that stymied the destructive downward leverage exerted by the discharging upper barrel, ultimately securing the barrels to the face of the action. Instead of adopting the preferred chopper lump bolting of side-by-sides, the innovative Anglos built ingenious bites and jointing trunnions into their over-under barrel flats and inside the action bar. By strategically placing bolts and bites midway between the barrels, British gunmakers thwarted the ever present barrel flip, while maintaining a low-profile action body. Unlike over-unders incorporating bolting lugs on the bottom barrel (i.e., the Browning Superposed and its worldwide progeny), which also increased the depth of the action, this type of bolting and jointing achieved three important objectives: it reduced the opening arc of the action, prevented gaping at the breech, and enabled the British to build a better-balanced, shallow-girthed over-under more in keeping with the streamlined attributes of a true game gun. These concepts were tested and perfected early in the twentieth century by the gunmaking wizardry of Woodward and Boss. Purdey further refined and strengthened these over-under precepts when it absorbed Woodward shortly after World War II. As such, the sublime Boss and Woodward/Purdey over-unders, though princely in price and scarce as rocking-horse dung, remain the sine qua non of vertically configured double guns. Like their side-by-side counterparts, these distinctly British over-unders have been imitated by gunmakers the world over. The classic-minded and gifted Italian gunmakers, especially, have adapted their functionally and esthetically beautiful over-unders to the British ideal.

Sensitive to the destructive forces that plague over-unders, the enterprising gunmakers of Germany and Austria carried bolting theory to its logical, if not inevitable, conclusion. Paralleling Greener's omnipresent crossbolt and L. C. Smith's legendary rotary bolt, which advantageously placed their bolting grips high on the frame, the Kersten-type crossbolt (twin bolting extensions on the top barrel), found on many Central European over-unders, is perhaps the strongest, most effective restraint yet devised for the recalcitrant top barrel. Unfortunately, the framework required to house such a bolting mechanism often sabotages any likelihood of sculpting a graceful action body, especially when combined with underlugs and a conventional hinge.

Wedding strength and beauty in a harmonious marriage is seldom achieved by over-under gunmakers on either side of the English Channel. This by no means denigrates Germanic efforts to build durable and shootable over-unders. Like much of their deep-relief engraving and artfully carved gunstocks, Prussian-proofed double guns make up in faultless engineering and unerring craftsmanship what they may lack in classic design. The last Merkel over-under I waltzed around a sporting clays course gave me a respectable score and a greater appreciation of German ergonomics. Handle a high-grade over-under built in Suhl, Germany, or Ferlach, Austria, and it will leave an indelible impression of quality and attention to detail that will compensate for a multitude of theoretical transgressions.

Attempts by the international sporting arms industry to mass-produce the meticulous hand finishing and fitting required to build a best-quality over-under have resulted in a mixed blessing of some affordable, yet less than svelte, double shotguns. Though all the parts can be machined to within a wisp of smoke, the synergy achieved by talented hands and discerning eyes cannot be completely duplicated by sophisticated technology. In this regard Boss and Purdey over-unders, along with their contemporary copies, will always command costly respect in the game gun marketplace. Those who can afford the privilege of owning a British "best" over-under will discover a joy in shooting that transcends barrel arrangement, and the insignificant detractors of a wider opening arc and crosswind resistance against the barrels.

Modern technology in the form of CAD/CAM (computer assisted design/computer assisted manufacture) software, digitized milling machinery, spark eroders, and the like have simplified the gunmaker's life considerably. A few of the larger, more progressive gun houses in England, and most of the forward-thinking gunmakers in Italy and the U.S., are making the capital investments required to reduce the labor-intensive tasks once performed by hand-weary artisans. Profiling, contouring, and fitting gun metal need no longer demand seemingly endless tedious work by bench-tethered action filers, lockmakers, and barrel strikers. In state-of-the-art facilities, gun parts can now be machined to space-age tolerances that require substantially less hand fitting and finishing to achieve best-quality results, and that mystical game gun synergy so eagerly sought by shooting sportsmen. Much to the chagrin of weight-conscious wingshooters, most American makers and importers offer over-unders built to absorb "magnum" shotshells and the specter of product liability suits. As a result, these overweight smoothbores are better suited to waterfowling and clay-target sports than the uplands.

Except for bolting and jointing, the manufacture of shallow-frame over-unders follows traditional game-gun production methods. Locks, stocks, and barrels are treated to the same time-honored tricks of the trade. Whether over-under or side-by-side, sidelock or boxlock, the size and weight of every double gun's action and barrels are determined by the distance between its centers (its firing pins). The greater the distance, the thicker the barrels, the larger the action body, the heavier the gun. Conversely, the centers on a lightweight game gun are usually placed as close together as gauge, balance, and safety will allow. Depending on wood density, the barreled action accounts for nearly 75 percent of a double gun's overall weight.

During the manufacturing process, over-under barrels require considerable attention at the breech end, with extractors, bolting, and jointing all formed within three inches of the standing breech. Before the barrels are joined, the rough tubes must be tested individually for straightness and imperfections. Each barrel is then locked in a vise and struck to the desired external taper from the breech end to the muzzles. Flats are filed on the breech end of each tube to facilitate precise barrel joining. The standing breech of the action is also filed and contoured to roughly accommodate barrel diameter and is further prepared for bolting and jointing. Before Boss-type over-under barrels are joined, the side pieces for the extractors must be filed and holes bored for the extractor rods. When classic double-gun barrels are made sans screw-in chokes (blasphemous toys of the nouveau riche), gunmakers can give the muzzles a trimmer appearance by filing flats on the barrels where they are joined at the muzzles. Such an esthetic treatment is not possible with screw-in chokes because of the metal required to install the choke tubes. Blunderbusses built to carve a groove in clay-target sports auger well for such screw-in appurtenances.

A set of barrels, regardless of chokes, is virtually worthless if it cannot deliver its payload accurately. To ensure that the tubes are joined and wired in perfect alignment, they are placed together on levelers (a $2\frac{1}{2}$-foot-length of trued steel with perfectly level runglike crossmembers at each end). When the tubes are absolutely level, they are wired together at the breech. The muzzle ends of the barrels are then pegged together with a clothespin-like clip. After rechecking their alignment, the tubes are fluxed at the muzzles and placed into the furnace, where they are brought to a rosy red glow for brazing. When cool, the barrels are cleaned and inspected for any heat distortion that may have occurred during the brazing process. If all is well, preparations are made to nail the ribs to the barrels. Over-unders normally require three ribs—two in the center of the barrels and one on top. On the more contemporary models, all three can be rakishly ventilated. Some even have removable center ribs like the Ruger Red wood and steel. However, when it comes to purely instinctive game shooting, the over-under is limited, primarily, to individuals with average to short appendages. By their very design, over-unders prevent long-armed shooters from taking a secure and comfortable grip beyond the forearm, as can be done on classic side-by-sides. On over-unders, the shooter's reach is limited by the length of the forearm. In a tight spot, demanding quick, accurate gun mounting and pointing, the over-under, even with a straight-hand grip, can be a handicap to the shooter of above-average stature. Whereas, in true game gun fashion, classic side-by-sides are fitted with inconsequential forearms that are mostly ignored by the instinctive shooter. Depending on the physical build of the shooter, the barrels are usually grasped forward of the forearm at a distance comfortable to the leading hand. Such an arrangement not only affords a secure grip and precise pointing, it also, by the placement of the thumb alongside the barrel, subconsciously forces the dominant eye to track the target. This hand-barrel relationship also encourages the leading hand to take a more active role in gun mounting, swing, and follow-through. It is a far more natural, less contrived response to wild-flushing, accelerating game birds. But, then again, those who own an over-under Boss, Purdey, Holland & Holland, or Euro/American facsimile, will delight in shooting holes in this argument, and rightfully so. After all, if shot well, a game gun by any other name is still a game gun.

In the tradition-steeped world of sporting shotguns, the twenty-first century will once again confront the welcome dilemma of choosing a "best" gun with barrels arranged atop or alongside one another. Maybe the only real solution for the serious wingshooter is to own at least one of each.

J. Woodward & Sons 12-gauge. Photo by William W. Headrick, courtesy of Lewis Drake & Associates.

9

THE GUN ROOM

I WALKED INTO THE IMMACULATE GUN ROOM and was immediately bathed in the smells of nitro solvent, Rangoon oil, chrome-tanned leather, boot dubbing, and pipe tobacco. My elderly host quietly handed me one of the many game guns I was privileged to fondle that cold winter morning, and began to reminisce about guns and gunmakers whose colorful legacy lives on despite their unfortunate demise. Churchill, Lancaster, Bonehill, Lang, Hollis, Boswell, Grant, Cogswell & Harrison, and Dickson of Great Britain; Baker, L. C. Smith, Lefever, Fox, Parker, and Ithaca of America; the litany of names conjured up a bygone era when labor was cheap and quality was high.

For hours that morning, we languished in the memory of the traditions and times that spawned such fine sporting arms. The room was a museum of sporting art and artifacts that celebrated one man's shooting life. His library of gun books was as extensive as his respect for the game birds and dogs that added satisfaction and character to his life. A relic of the past, he, too, would soon pass from a contemporary world that seems more preoccupied with the high-tech things of man than with the wild spirit of the land. His next of kin would squabble over his worldly remains, divide the spoils of his sporting life, and liquidate the substance of his dreams at the local pawn shop.

I'm glad I knew this man. He still lives on in the heart of every hunter who appreciates oil-finished walnut and engraved gun steel, who thrills to staunch dogs and wild birds, who cares more about playing the game to its fullest and not just filling a game bag, and who treasures moments afield with companions who can tell how to hunt a promising covert without saying a word. He is someone's father, uncle, or son who is keeping the tradition of Southern quail hunting, New England grouse hunting, Midwestern woodcock hunting, or English driven-bird shooting, alive.

One of the old gentleman's guns that survived the estate sale reposes quietly in its burgundy, billiard-cloth-lined, oak-and-leather case in a back corner of the closet in my den. And because the old gentleman once told me you could tell a lot about a man by the way he cared for his guns, my humble gun room is decked out with enough accoutrements and cleaning equipment to keep the old game gun shooting true for a few more generations.

If I breathe deeply enough I can still smell, almost taste, the rich aromas that dwelled in the old gentleman's gun room. It is the kind of room the world needs more of.

OAK AND LEATHER

A good game gun deserves a good case. Today, a traditional gun case of oak and leather will cost more than a game gun itself did just a few decades ago. Made by hand from densely grained white or red oak and high-quality saddle leather, an oak-and-leather case is still the proper treatment for a high-grade gun.

Designed for durability during the days when travel itself was often an adventure, these cases survive today because they combine romance with protection of both the gun and the gun owner. Oak-

~ THE GUN ROOM ~

The complete game gunner is as fastidious about accoutrements as he is about the selection of chokes.

and-leather cases are normally fitted with French-rolled compartments for snap caps, oil bottles, turnscrews, chamber brushes, etc. Stock and barrel assemblies are fitted so precisely in these cases that the gun is well protected from jarring mishaps frequently encountered during transport.

  For esthetics, transport purposes, and brief periods of storage, the traditional oak-and-leather case affords maximum protection. It also serves as a self-contained cleaning station to keep the gun properly maintained at home or in the field. With its gleaming brass corners and hardware, an oak-and-leather case, complete with leather-trimmed canvas cover, can weigh as much as three times the gun it was built to protect.

Vintage oak-and-leather cases often exhibit heavily pigmented, vegetable-dyed leather bonded to the wood with animal glue. Along with the oak wainscoting, pine was most frequently used to construct the upper lid and lower compartment of the case, although mahogany is the choice of a few master case-builders who feel its relative inertness prevents frame warpage over the years.

As the mode of transportation became more civilized, the valise-style leather carrying case (VC) and the motorcase gained prominence. The leather corners of the VC case made it less cumbersome and more convenient for automobile travel. In addition to their light weight, VC cases are often more streamlined and carry fewer accessories than the traditional oak-and-leather case.

A motorcase differs from a VC case in that it is more square than rectangular in shape and is opened from one or both ends. Often made from top-grain leather, motorcases were compactly built to stow more easily in the skimpy trunks of early motorcars. A disassembled double gun is slipped into the motorcase much in the same fashion it is placed in a leg-o-mutton case. Some motorcases require that the butt section be placed in one end and the barrel assembly in the other.

Leg-o-mutton leather cases also provide adequate protection for take-down guns. Many a fine Parker, Fox, and L. C. Smith continue to be toted to and from the coverts in these cloth-lined, oil-treated cases. Unless built with an external compartment, the leg-o-mutton case has no provisions for cleaning equipment except perhaps for simple "pull-through" mops and jags.

For convenience, and to prevent unnecessary wear and tear, many bird hunters slip their prized double guns into a full length, fleece-lined canvas case as they travel from one covert to the next. However, a shotgun stored in such a case for a prolonged period is headed for trouble. The fleece lining is a great moisture trap and can cause surface rusting on an uncleaned gun almost overnight.

Ideally, all guns should be stored in a climate-controlled gun cabinet in either a horizontal or muzzle-down position. Otherwise, gravity takes its inevitable toll on the jaws of the stock from well-oiled guns stored in the typical butt-down position.

Oil- and solvent-soaked inletting increases the possibility of splitting and cracking of gun wood. Animal and petroleum-based oils are particularly harmful to stock wood. It seems a common quirk of American logic that if a little lubrication on a mechanism is good, a lot must be better. It is a dangerous philosophy. Fine guns should be treated to a thin film of high-grade lubricant to ensure optimal performance season after season.

SNAP CAPS

For those who enjoy dry-firing their game guns at imaginary targets on gun room walls, snap caps are indispensable items indeed. Nickel-plated and fitted with replaceable rubber primers to absorb shock from the firing pins, snap caps are made in sizes from 4-gauge to .410 both in England and the U.S. As traditional as tea and crumpets, English snap caps are still readily available through the larger gun houses whose company names are also engraved or stamped on the head of the dummy cartridges.

Nickel-plated snap cap and oil bottles give the discriminating gun owner added pride in ownership.

Though considered by some a needless prestige item, quality snap caps enable a shooter to maintain familiarity with his gun during the long off-season. And while some double gun makers may contend that dry-firing on empty chambers will not damage the firing pins, I tend to agree with the old school that says, "Why take the risk?" This bit of wisdom rings especially true when it comes to vintage sidelock doubles. Locating the proper firing pins for one of these old relics, as well as a qualified gunsmith to install them, is a search many hunters would prefer to forgo, particularly at the height of bird season.

OIL BOTTLES

The gleaming elegance of square and round oil bottles has graced trunk cases and gun rooms for generations. As practical as they are attractive, nickel-plated or pewter oil bottles provide a stable reservoir for a gunner's favorite lubricant. Whether filled with Rangoon, Three-In-One, whale oil, or a new space-age lubricant, chrome bottles, with their lid-attached applicators, add a touch of class to gun cleaning and maintenance.

Some shooters make the mistake of storing nitro solvent in oil bottles, perhaps assuming that nickel is impervious to its cleaning action. However, the inside surface of an oil bottle is not nickel, but brass. Over a period of time, the brass will react with the solvent, at first diluting its effectiveness, and eventually neutralizing it entirely. Repeated attempts to store solvent in oil bottles will erode the brass to the degree that the bottle will become useless.

Currently, oil bottles are offered in a variety of sizes, with the most popular being the square $1\frac{1}{2}$-inch and 2-inch sizes. The purchaser also has the option of having his favorite gunmaker's name inscribed on the lid, usually at no extra charge. Tradition dies hard in England, so one can expect these handsome containers to be available for quite some time. I am also aware of one U.S. company that is gearing up for the production of a variety of nickel-plated oil bottles and snap caps. Samples I have seen are of a quality in keeping with England's high standards.

To overcome the drawbacks encountered with solvent storage, traditional glass bottles can still be obtained in configurations as attractive as they are functional. One may have to search a little harder to find a high-quality glass bottle, but they are worth the effort.

STRIKER BOTTLES

Traditionally fashioned from elephant-tusk ivory, these handy little containers have been coveted by maharajas and white hunters alike. A repository for spare firing pins ("strikers"), springs, screws, etc., these bottles are usually associated with other ivory-trimmed accoutrements found in an oak-and-leather case built to accompany an English "best" sidelock double gun or rifle.

With the great demands being made on legal ivory today, along with the worldwide hue and cry to stop elephant poaching, carved and engraved striker bottles are a luxury the gun trade may soon have to live without. However, by virtue of their scarcity, collectors will no doubt rescue a few for future generations of shotgun fanciers. Whether made from ivory or nickel-plated brass, every serious shotgun man should have at least one striker bottle in his gun room.

TURNSCREWS

During the days when the sun never set on the British Empire, it was imperative that early explorers, traders, and hunters be prepared to clean and repair their own guns. To fill that need, a complete set of turnscrews (screwdrivers) were individually shaped and honed by the gunmaker to match the pin (screw) slots of every game gun destined for distant shores. Their necessity was minimized some with Holland & Holland's and Westley Richards' development of hand-detachable locks, but quality turnscrews are still highly prized by discriminating gun owners. Fashioned from high-carbon steel, these tools, when properly used, prevent the unsightly disfiguration of pin slots which often occurs when improper screwdrivers are used.

Handles for turnscrews have been produced from a variety of materials ranging from rosewood to walnut to Indian horn, with ebony being the most common. Anyone fortunate enough to own a set of hand-carved, ivory-handled turnscrews can strut a little even if he doesn't own a game gun. High-quality turnscrews of present manufacture can be purchased over the counter, giving the gun owner the option of honing the blades to fit his particular gun needs.

Nestled end to end in French-fitted compartments of an oak-and-leather case, custom-crafted turnscrews offer gunners practicality as well as pride of ownership. In part, they reflect and perpetuate the same proud heritage as the simple hand tools used to craft a best-quality game gun.

BUSHING TURNSCREW

Although not as common as regular turnscrews, the bushing turnscrew is indispensable to the man who owns a game gun with removable firing-pin bushings. Screwed flush into the standing breech, firing-pin bushings are made with two- or three-hole patterns. The prongs on a bushing turnscrew are designed to correspond with these hole patterns, enabling the hunter to replace a firing pin while in the field if necessary.

CARTRIDGE EXTRACTORS

Looking more like a utensil from the kitchen than a gun tool, cartridge extractors are vestiges from black powder and early smokeless-powder days when imprecise loading techniques often caused soft brass cartridge heads to lodge in the chambers. Cartridge extractors functioned much like a carpenter's claw hammer to extract stubborn shells the gun's ejectors could not expel. Although seldom needed for today's modern ammunition, a cartridge extractor in the field would sure beat trying to ramrod a stuck cartridge from the chamber with a hastily cut willow switch.

CLEANING ROD

Even though aluminum and plastic perform bore-cleaning chores quite nicely, there is something about a brass-trimmed ebony or oak cleaning rod that makes the task more enjoyable. Usually found neatly stored beneath the barrel assembly in an oak-and-leather case, classic, two-piece or three-piece rods can still be bought individually from various upscale mail-order houses in the United States and Great Britain. There are also a select number of walnut-cased cleaning kits that contain wood and brass rods. Admittedly, such cleaning rods are more for show than anything else, but the warmth of wood and touch of brass do add a dimension to double-gun ownership no plastic could ever duplicate.

Most wooden cleaning rods are varnished, but some gun owners prefer a hand-rubbed oil finish, in keeping with the tradition of a London "best" gun.

CHAMBER BRUSH

A great many gun owners today are rediscovering the utility and necessity of owning a horsehair bristle chamber brush. With the advent of plastic shotshells, many high-grade double guns have succumbed to rusted and pitted chambers. Because of the water resistant properties of plastic, debris and moisture can be trapped in the pores of the chamber walls, which can result in corrosion. A quality chamber brush can remove this plastic buildup with a few brisk strokes. Lacking a good chamber brush, a phosphor bronze brush one gauge larger than the bore will accomplish the same result. Chamber brushes, like chambermaids, can be as comely as you desire. Some chamber brushes even sport ivory handles and gilded shafts, but, above all else, they should be able to clean a chamber thoroughly.

PHOSPHOR BRONZE BRUSHES

Few things will scrub a bore to mirror brightness better than a good quality phosphor bronze brush. With the help of a brand name nitro solvent, it removes both plastic wad and lead buildup with very little effort.

Some feel it is unnecessary to use a bronze brush every time the bores are cleaned, especially with today's modern ammunition. I disagree. Shiny, rust-free bores are the result of a religious application of elbow grease, nitro solvent, and phosphor bronze brushing.

A common mistake made by gunners when cleaning is to impart a back-and-forth action to the brush while it is still in the bore. This method eventually fatigues the bristles, resulting in a flat-sided brush. I have worn out more than a few that way myself. Ideally, the brush should be spiraled down from the breech end of the gun, through the bore, and out the muzzle. If more than one pass is needed, the brush should be unscrewed from the cleaning rod, the rod withdrawn from the bore, the brush reattached, and the process repeated.

HAND GUARDS

To the British, forearms on game guns serve only two purposes: to house the ejector mechanism and to hold the gun together. Beyond these functions, the fore-end is totally ignored by most English shooters. Because the gunner's leading arm is almost fully extended when shooting, the English shooter simply cradles the barrels in his hand. Thus, the hand guard was designed to insulate the hand from hot barrels during prolonged shooting sessions on driven birds.

Made from spring steel, with usually brown or black Moroccan leather coverings, hand guards are proportioned by gauge and slide freely from fore-end to muzzle to accommodate the shooter's natural reach—a free-floating version of an American beavertail forearm.

TOMPONS

A seldom-seen accessory used for the temporary protection of a double gun's bores are the felt-covered plugs called tompons. Sized to fit the various gauges, tompons prevent dust and other debris from collecting in

Barrel tompons and hand guards.

the muzzles of guns that are stored in the upright position. Tompons are connected by a brass or chrome half-ring that allows easy insertion and removal.

Fly fishermen use simple wood or cork tompons to protect the female ferrules of expensive split cane rods during storage, and shotgun tompons work much the same way. However, shotgun tompons should never be left in the barrels of a gun that is to be stored indefinitely. The vagaries of humidity are such that if the barrels are not allowed to "breathe," moisture trapped in the bores by the tompons will cause corrosion. Used with discretion, tompons can be helpful items for gun owners who display large collections of double shotguns.

RECOIL PADS

Before the popular ventilated recoil pads cornered the market, solid red rubber pads, such as the Hawkins and Silvers, graced the higher-grade game guns produced earlier in the century in America and England. Handsomely styled with black spacers, these conservative pads did not detract from a gun's appearance as do some of the ventilated configurations now offered. Granted, the cushioning properties of these old pads wasn't all that great (they had a tendency to harden with age), but they were much more surer on the shoulder than many of today's squirmy offerings.

The Silvers pad even sported an attractively tapered protrusion at the top of its black spacer which required inletting into the buttstock. It gave the pad a built-in rather than just an added-on look.

Since many stocks are padded to gain length of pull for the shooter, and not particularly to reduce recoil, the few solid pads currently available are still the purist's choice.

And for upland bird hunters, whose success depends greatly on a smooth-mounting gun, the seldom seen leather-faced and leather-covered pads are preferable as they do not catch or bind on clothing on their way to the shoulder. Trouble is, there are few gunsmiths around who are capable of properly finishing such pads.

The old way may not always be the best way, but it is hard for even the most progressive in the shooting fraternity to dispute logic gleaned from generations of practical experience afield. The old ways, unfortunately, continue to fall victim to labor-saving, cost-cutting techniques that apply more to widgets and baubles than to a well-made game gun.

GUN CLOTHS

Like an understanding wife, a good gun cloth is a joy to the game gunner. It not only prevents rust-blued barrels from rusting, it also gives the hunter an opportunity to stay well acquainted with his shotgun. Whether an oil-soaked chamois or fleece-lined pad, gun cloths can add years to the looks and luster of a fine shotgun.

For ease of cleaning and metal protection, I prefer a fresh silicone gun cloth. The silicone is harmless to wood, and the mere heat from one's hand helps to spread it to those hard-to-reach areas around the fences, top rib of the barrels, and engraved surfaces of a gun.

The only mishap I ever experienced with a silicone cloth was a result of my own stupidity. One winter, I wrapped a frequently used silicone cloth around the breech end of an extra set of barrels and tucked them away in a luggage-style case. When I inspected the gun the following summer and removed the cloth, the barrels looked as if someone had run across the breech with track shoes. The pitting was not only extensive, it was so deep that the barrels could not be reblued without carding off the gunmaker's markings as well. The wisdom of frequent gun inspection finally soaked in, and I learned that a gun cloth should be stored in its own container, never wrapped around gun metal. Obviously, silicone wasn't the only thing present in that cloth; perspiration from my hand trapped in the cloth provided all the salt needed to permanently scar an otherwise beautiful gun.

Silicone gun cloths are relatively inexpensive, so it pays to keep a supply on hand rather than overworking one beyond its limits. Many hunters salvage old silicone cloths by spraying them with WD-40, G-96, and the like.

Whatever style cloth the hunter chooses, the lubricant it carries must be viable. If it is oil, it must be applied sparingly; oil applied too liberally can also, under certain conditions, trap moisture against metal and promote rusting. Proper gun-cloth use, coupled with frequent and vigilant gun inspections, will ensure a harmonious reunion of hunter and unblemished gun every bird season.

CARE AND CLEANING

My desk may be somewhat cluttered, my clothes unkempt, and my bank account beleaguered, but come hell or high water, I keep my guns as clean as humanly possible. It is somehow psychologically comforting to know that the first two shots from my double will exit bores that have been cleaned to mirror brightness. Nothing disturbs me more than to pick up a classic double in fine condition externally only to find its bores covered with lead fouling, burnt powder, or, worse yet, cavernous pits. Unless one is far removed from civilization for an extended period without cleaning equipment, there is no excuse for pitted shotgun bores.

There was a school of thought some years ago that believed pitted bores actually improved shotgun patterns. Some old-timers were so steadfast in their belief that they urinated down the bores of their doubles to promote pitting in hopes of achieving the desired friction effect on the shot column. Whether this gained them anything more than pitted bores is an entirely moot point today. Modern ammunition is ballistically superior to any such dubious bore alterations.

If nothing else, a thoroughly cleaned gun indicates a healthy sign of respect for a very deadly instrument. Like brushing his teeth after meals, the disciplined bird hunter will take time to clean his shotgun after every outing, regardless of how foot-weary or famished.

Over the years, I have distilled bore cleaning into a fairly simple procedure. After disassembling the gun, I stuff a white facial tissue (unscented and the coarser and cheaper, the better) into each barrel at the breech. This forms a cleaning plug of sorts that, when pushed through the bore, removes most of the burnt powder residue. Precut flannel patches are nice, but they are also costly. Even when purchased in bulk rolls, the flannel still must be cut into patches, which is bothersome. Facial tissues adapt themselves well to any bore diameter and are readily available.

After the initial push-through of tissue, I attach a phosphor bronze brush to a cleaning rod, immerse it in Hoppes No. 9, and thoroughly scrub each bore. (If there is any solvent on the market today better than old Hoppes "Aromatic" No. 9, I have yet to discover it.) In addition to loosening any lead buildup, the brushing also deposits a liberal quantity of solvent throughout each bore. I will often allow the Hoppes to work for an hour or more before sopping it up with fresh wads of tissue. If I plan on storing the gun for any length of time, I brush another application of solvent through the bores and leave it overnight. It is surprising how much more fouling will weep from the barrels' pores during this time.

For prolonged storage between seasons, I repeat the cleaning process three or four times within the first few months of storage. After I am convinced no appreciable fouling remains, I use a cotton mop of proper bore diameter to apply a thin film of high-grade oil to the bores—lots of fuss, maybe, but no rust.

Proper lubrication is essential to the longevity of every game gun. Top levers, underbolts, hinge pins, chopper lumps, lock parts, and even the safety slide all require lubrication. Even though the polymer-based, space-age lubricants have their devotees, I am convinced that Mother Nature has already supplied a superior lubricant in the form of sperm whale oil. It has been used by the scientific community for decades to lubricate intricate measuring and testing mechanisms. Bearing surfaces treated to a thin film of whale oil remain virtually friction-free under the heaviest of use. The oil can also be used to break in the action of a new double gun that is often stiff and otherwise difficult to operate until a few hundred rounds have been put through it.

Every time I clean my sidelock, I reflect on the old gentleman's advice on gun care. He applied his simple "keep it clean" philosophy to every facet of his sporting life. From his elegant collection of sporting arms to his strict outdoor code of ethics, the old gentleman knew well that hunting was a whole lot more than putting game on the table; it was a sacred way of life. We may have exchanged our Clovis points for game guns, but it is still the hunt that binds us to the land. If we remain close to the good earth and conserve and nurture its diverse habitats, our gun rooms will be havens for future generations of hunters. It is a privilege and an obligation worth fighting for.

GLOSSARY

annealing. A process used to soften gun metal for engraving or repair purposes.

back-action. A type of sidelock mechanism where the mainspring and other lock parts are positioned to the rear of the sideplate.

banknote engraving. A very delicate, yet distinctive style of engraving created by the subtle light and dark shading of simple hand gravers. Its near photographic quality makes it well suited for game scenes and other visual motifs.

bar-action. A type of sidelock mechanism whose mainspring protrudes laterally along the bar of the action (side of the receiver).

barrel flats. The flattened portion of the breech end of the barrels that closes on the water table of the receiver.

beavertail fore-end/forearm. A broad, elongated gripping surface contoured along the barrels to provide the leading hand with better support and control of the shotgun.

bend. Often referred to as drop, bend is the distance (measured in inches) the buttstock tapers away or drops from the plane of the barrels. Bend at the forward portion of the stock (comb) varies from 1⅛ inch to 1¾ inch, while bend at the back of the stock (heel) varies from 1⅞ inch to 3 inches.

"best" gun. A term coined by the British to describe a top-of-the-line game gun.

blank. A rough-cut piece of walnut from which a shotgun stock and forearm are produced.

bluing. Sometimes referred to as "browning" or "blacking" by the gun trade, bluing is a process that coats bare metal with a protective blue sheen. Whether hot blue, cold blue, or rust blue, bluing remains the standard treatment for trigger guards and barrels.

boxlock. A double-gun mechanism designed late in the nineteenth century that houses the locks within the body of the receiver.

bulino. Italian engraving. See Banknote.

bushings. Small, circular firing-pin plates that screw into the face of the standing breech to facilitate easy repair and replacement of firing pins.

bushing turnscrew. A two- or three-pronged hand tool used to install and remove bushings.

butt. Rear section of the shotgun that mounts against the shoulder.

buttstock. The entire portion of walnut comprising the jaws, grip, comb, and butt, commonly referred to as the "stock."

cartridge extractor. A hand tool used to extract spent cartridges stuck in the shotgun's chambers.

casehardening. A process used to heat-strengthen and color gunmetal.

cast-off. The lateral bend of the buttstock (measured in fractions of an inch) to the right of the center of the barrels to compensate for the anatomy of right-handed shooters.

cast-on. The reverse of cast-off.

chamber. That portion of the breech end of a shotgun barrel that receives and supports the cartridge.

Glossary

chamber brush. A hand tool fitted with a circular bristled brush for scrubbing and cleaning shotgun chambers.

checkering. Diamonds of varying size and design cut into the hand (grip) of the buttstock and forearm.

cheekpiece. A surplus of wood sculptured into the comb of the buttstock to provide a broad rest for the shooter's cheek.

choke. The degree of constriction built in at the muzzle end of the barrels to control the density of shot pellets at a given distance.

chopper lump. A commonly used method for joining barrels (with integral barrel lumps) into a solid unit that is machined and hand filed to bolt securely to the shotgun's receiver.

cocking indicators. Protruding pins on sidelock and boxlock shotguns and rifles that serve as visual and tactile indicators of the cocking status of the locks.

comb. The top forward portion of the buttstock.

crossbolt. A device usually consisting of a large, tapered bolt (housed in the fence of the receiver) that cams through a barrel extension to lock the barrels firmly to the breech.

Damascus steel. An early shotgun barrelmaking process pioneered by Belgian gunmakers where strands of iron were hammered and welded around a steel mandrel to create ornate barrels for use with black-powder shotgun shells.

deep-relief engraving. An engraving technique requiring substantial metal removal by hammer and chisel and hand gravers to create bold scroll patterns, game scenes, oak-leaf clusters, and other designs on sidelocks, receivers, and barrels.

doll's head. A round or rectangular top rib extension that fits snugly into a slot milled into the top of the standing breech to help secure the barrels to the breech.

dovetail. A method for joining the barrel lumps of a side-by-side shotgun by dovetailing one lump into the other.

drilling. A firearm combining a side-by-side shotgun and single-shot rifle. Popular in Germany, where small and big game are encountered during the same hunt.

drop. See Bend.

drop spec fine scroll. Delicate hand engraving requiring numerous cuts for each scroll. Usually reserved for "best" guns.

ejectors. Closely fitted to the bottom of the barrel breech, ejectors kick out fired cartridges and elevate unfired shells when the shotgun is opened. The ejector mechanism is housed in the fore-end assembly.

Englishing. The process of adjusting side-by-side barrels so they pattern properly downrange.

engraving. Ranging from simple to ornate, engraving is an artistic embellishment applied either by hand or machine to the external metal surfaces of a shotgun or rifle.

extractors. Closely fitted to the bottom of the barrel breech, extractors simply elevate spent and unfired cartridges when the shotgun is opened.

fences. A term carried over from the old hammer-gun days referring to the rounded barrel bolsters on top of the standing breech.

firing pins (strikers). Floating or rebounding pins that strike and detonate shotshell primers.

fluid steel. Barrels that are forged, machined, and bored from a continuous bar of alloy steel.

fore-end/forearm. A shotgun's forward assembly that attaches to the knuckle of the receiver and bottom of the barrels.

fore-end loop (hanger). A hook-like appendage brazed to the bottom of the barrels that attaches to the forearm assembly.

funeral gun. A side-by-side shotgun whose metal parts have all been blued or blacked. Also referred to as a "black widow" gun.

gold inlay. Part of the engraving process that weds gold game animals, dogs, monograms, borders, etc., with gun steel.

hammers (tumblers). Tempered metal gun parts housed in sidelocks or boxlocks that drive the firing pins into cartridge primers when the triggers are pulled.

hand. An English term referring to the wrist or grip of the buttstock.

Glossary

hand protector. A leather-covered steel accessory that slides over a side-by-side's barrels to protect the leading hand from barrel heat. Frequently used on English doubles sporting splinter forends.

head space. A term used to describe the space created between the standing breech and the cartridge head slot at the breech end of the chamber.

heel. The top rear portion of the buttstock.

hinge pin. The large pin at the joint of the receiver upon which the forward lug of the barrels pivots.

hinged trigger. The forward trigger of a double-triggered shotgun that articulates frontward if bumped upon recoil by the index finger after the rear trigger is pulled. Also referred to as an articulated trigger.

inletting. The careful removal of wood or metal to accept a shotgun's working mechanisms.

in the white. Gunmetal which has not been case hardened or blued.

leg-o-mutton. A leather case shaped somewhat like a leg of mutton that is designed to carry a disassembled double gun or repeater.

locks. Mechanisms that discharge the shotgun when the triggers are pulled.

lockplate. The part of a sidelock shotgun that contains the firing mechanism.

lock time. The quickness with which the locks discharge the gun after the triggers are pulled.

monoblock. A method of double-gun barrel assembly that involves the insertion of sleeved barrels into an integral breech block.

motorcase. A squarish, double-ended leather case used to protect disassembled shotguns during transport.

oak-and-leather case. An oak-framed, leather-covered, brass-cornered, luggage-style gun case used by traditional game gun makers to house a "best" gun and its accoutrements.

pistol grip. A style of shotgun grip that positions the rear hand perpendicular to the barrels.

pitch. The amount of downward influence exerted on a shotgun's barrels affected by the bend of the buttstock and the angle of the cut at the butt.

proof house. Found in England and numerous European countries, proof houses were established by government to ensure a standard of firearms quality and safety.

proof load. A load usually half again as powerful as the heaviest commercial load, used by proof houses to test the strength and integrity of a barreled action.

pull (length of pull). The measurement taken in inches between the front trigger and the center of the butt end of the stock.

receiver. Also known as the action body, the receiver is the heavy metal anvil on which the barrels, lock, and forend iron are mounted.

rib. A tapered ramp brazed between the barrels of a double gun.

rose-and-scroll engraving. A style of engraving using scrolls and rose bouquets preferred by classic gunmakers.

safety. A thumb-operated device usually found on the action tang of a double gun used to help prevent the accidental discharge of a shotgun.

side-clips. Small scallop-like protrusions on the standing breech that inlet to the barrels to retard lateral movement of the barrels during discharge.

sidelock. A type of lock mechanism that internalized the hammers found on the old hammer guns while at the same time improving lock time and safety.

sideplate. See Lockplate. Dummy sideplates are sometimes used in conjunction with boxlock guns to emulate the sidelock action.

sight picture. Refers to the shooter's vision as it relates to the top rib, barrels, bead, and target after the double gun is mounted.

single-selective trigger. A single trigger that can be activated to select the desired barrel sequence.

sleeving. The process of inserting barrels into a breech block.

snap caps. Dummy cartridges used during dry-firing practice.

splinter forearm/fore-end. An English-style forearm that uses just enough wood to surround the metal parts of the fore-end.

Glossary

sporting clays. A clay-bird game that simulates the various shots encountered when upland bird and waterfowl hunting.

standing breech. The upright portion of the action body that receives the breech end of the barrels.

straight grip. A buttstock grip preferred by the British that positions the rear hand parallel to the barrels.

striker bottle. A container for spare firing pins (strikers).

tang. The rear portion of the receiver back strap that houses the safety mechanism.

third grip. A small extension at the breech end of the barrels that fits into a slot milled into the face of the standing breech. When the gun is closed, the extension is held by an over-lever that helps prevent downward flexing of the barrels at the breech.

toe. The slightly pointed, bottom rear portion of the buttstock.

tompons. Protective, felt-covered plugs inserted at the muzzle end of the barrels.

top lever. The thumb-activated lever on top of the receiver that opens the shotgun's action.

trigger-guard bow and strap. A two-piece assembly that protects the triggers. The bow attaches to the bottom of the receiver and its connected strap inlets along the bottom of the buttstock's grip.

try-gun. An adjustable gun used by the gunmaker to custom fit gunstock dimensions to the shooter.

turnscrews. Screwdrivers especially built to match the screw slots of a game gun.

underbolt. Activated by the top lever, the underbolt cams into the barrel lug slots when the gun is closed.

valise carrying case (V.C.). A lightweight, leather-covered, luggage-style case used to transport and protect disassembled double guns.

water table. The flat portion of the receiver (action body) that runs parallel to the barrels.

wrist. That portion of the buttstock also referred to as the hand or grip.

Gun Dealers, Makers, and Master Craftsmen

DEALERS

Fieldsport
3313 W. South Airport Rd.
Traverse City, MI 49684
616-933-0767
Fax: 616-933-0768

Galazan
P. O. Box 1692
New Britain, CT 06051-1692
203-225-6581
Fax: 203-832-8707

Game Fair Ltd.
99 Whitebridge Rd., Suite 105
Nashville, TN 37205
615-353-0602

Griffin & Howe, Inc.
36 W. 44th Street, Suite 1011
New York, NY 10036
212-921-0980

Holland & Holland, Ltd.
50 E. 57th Street
New York, NY 10022
212-752-7755
Fax: 212-752-6805

The Hunter Collection
3000 Zelda Road
Montgomery, AL 36106
334-244-9586
Fax: 334-270-4134

Jaqua's
900 E. Bigelow Ave.
Findlay, OH 45840
419-422-0912
Fax: 419-422-3575

William Larkin Moore & Co.
31360 Via Colinas, Suite 109
Westlake Village, CA 91360

Orvis
10 River Road
Manchester, VT 05254

Don Thompson
W10745 County Road J
Lodi, WI 53555
608-592-5420

Woodcock Hill
Rd. #1 Box 147
Benton, PA 17814
717-864-3242
Fax: 717-864-3232
www.shooters.com/woodcock

GUNMAKERS

Beretta U.S.A.
17601 Indian Head Hwy.
Accokeek, MD 20607

Boss & Company
London, England

Browning Arms
Route 1
Morgan, UT 84050

Champlin Firearms, Inc.
Box 3191
Enid, OK 73701

Connecticutt Shotgun Mfg.
P. O. Box 1692
35 Woodland Street
New Britain, CT 06051-1692
203-225-6682
Fax: 203-832-8707

John Dickson & Son
Edinburgh, Scotland

Famars, Abbiatico & Salvinelli
Via Cinelli 29
Gardone V.T.
(Brescia) 25063, Italy

J. Fanzoj
P. O. Box 25
Ferlach 9170, Austria

Armi FERLIB
46 Via Costa
25063 Gardone V.T., Brescia, Italy

Auguste Francotte & Cie, S.A.
61 Mont St. Martin
4000 Liège, Belgium

Armas Garbi
Urki 12
Eibar (Guipuzcoa), Spain

Gun Dealers, Makers, and Master Craftsmen

Georges Granger
66 Cours Fauriel
42 St. Etienne, France

Holland & Holland, Ltd.
33 Bruton Street
London W1X8JS, England

Franz Sodia Jogdgewehrfabrik
Schulhausegasse 14
9170 Ferlach, (Karnten), Austria

Perazzi U.S.A., Inc.
206 S. George Street
Rome, NY 13440

James Purdey & Sons, Ltd.
Audley House
57-58 Audley Street
London W1Y6ED, England

Westley Richards
Grange Road, Bournbrook
Birmingham B29 6AR, England

F. Ili Rizzini
25060 Magno di Gardone V.T.
(Bs.), Italy

W. & C. Scott Ltd.
Tame Road
Birmingham B67HS, England

U.S. Repeating Arms Company
275 Winchester Avenue
P. O. Box 30-300
New Haven, CT 06511

Perugini Visini & Co. s.r.l.
Via Camprelle 126
25080 Nuvolera (Bs.), Italy

Winchester International
Olin Corp.
Alton, IL 62024

MASTER CRAFTSMEN

Stockmakers

David Trevallion
9 Old Mt. Rd.
Cape Neddick, ME 03902
207-361-1130

Fred Wenig
P. O. Box 249 - Old Bank Bldg.
103 N. Market
Lincoln, MO 65338
816-547-3334
Fax: 816-547-2881

Dave Wills
2776 Brevard Ave.
Montgomery, AL 36109
334-272-0075

Barrelmakers

Kirk Merrington
207 Sierra Road
Kerrville, TX 78028
210-367-2937
Fax: 210-367-2950

Gunsmiths

Dennis Potter
13960 Boxhorn Drive
Muskego, WI 53150
414-425-4830

Engravers

Winston G. Churchill
R.F.D. Box 29B
Proctorsville, VT 05153
802-226-7772

Ron Collings
1006 Cielita Linda Drive
Vista, CA 92083
619-758-8347
Fax: 619-758-1906

C. Hunt Turner
618 S. Gore Ave.
Webster Grove, MO 63119
314-961-8209

Firearms Restoration

Larry DelGrego & Son
85 North 5th Ave.
Ilion, NY 13357
315-894-8754

Nick Makinson
R.R. 3 Komoka
Ontarion, Canada NOL 1RO
519-471-5462

Doug Turnbull
6426 County Road 30
P. O. Box 471
Bloomfiled, NY 14469
716-657-6338
www:http://gunshop.com/dougt.htm

INDEX

A
action body, 48-53, 161
    back-action, 49, 52
    bar-action, 49, 52
    identifying type, 52
    measurement, 49, 161
    production, 60 (illustr.)
action flats, 52
action filer, 49
Ambercrombie & Fitch, 137
American "best" guns, 4, 9, 26, 115-130
American gunmaking
    history of, 117, 118, 120, 126, 128, 130
American shotgunning,
    history of, 5, 9-10
annealing, 67

Appleby, Malcolm, 103
Arizabalaga gun, 144
Arrieta guns, 142-144
Austrian gunmaking, 5, 133, 146-147, 160
automatic ejectors, 54
AyA guns, 140

B
Baker guns, 130, 169
banknote engraving, 94. *See also* bulino engraving
barrel blanks, 34-35
    chopper lump, 34, 35, 52
    dovetail, 34
    monoblock, 35
barrel flats, 42
barrel length, 48
barrel sequence, 24-25

barrelmaking, 34-48
  history of, 42-43
  standards, 43-4
  specifications, 41, 161
    resilience of, 36-38
    grainstructure, 36, 52
  procedures
    barrel choking, 44-46
      recessed, 44
      reverse, 44
      swage method, 44-45
      traditional method, 44-45
      English standards of, 45-46
    barrel reaming, 41
    barrel striking, 39
    boring, 34
    burnishing, 46
    casehardening, 47
    cold rust-bluing, 46-47
    lapping, 41
    "nailing the ribs," 40
    proofing, 42-44
    "ringing the barrels," 4
    spill boring, 35-36
    truing operation, 34
Belgian gunmaking, 133, 136-138
bend, 16. See also cast
Beretta guns, 148, 149
Bernardelli guns, 148, 149
"best" guns,
  anatomy of, 2
  English, 3, 9, 53
  vintage, American, 9
Birmingham Proof House, 42
black widow gun, 47-48
bolting, 67-69
  double underlug, 68
  flexibility of, 68
  grip, 68
  Purdey design, 67-68
  L. C. Smith rotary bolt design, 69
Bonehill guns, 169
bore cleaning, 181-182

boring machines, 36
Boss guns, 3, 155, 158, 159
  single trigger over-unders, 165
Boswell guns, 169
Boutet guns, 134
boxlocks, 128
  over-under, 27
  self-opening, 56
brazing, 162
breech problems, 68
  with Winchester Model 21, 69
breechloading shotguns,
  advent of, 158
Brescia, Italy, 133, 147
British gunmaking, 1-5, 8, 13-14, 22, 24-25, 41-43, 53-54, 56, 154-155, 157-160
British shotgunning, history of, 5
Browning Arms, 138
    Japanese-made, 151, 152
    A5 autoloader, 5, 138
    BSS Sporter, 152
    "One of One" Superposed, 163 (illustr.)
    Superposed, 159
    over-under, 138
    sidelock, 152
Buckingham, Nash, 128
bulino engraving, 101 (illustr.), 102-103. See also banknote
bushing turnscrew, 176
buttstock, 26

C
cartridge extractors, 176
casehardening, 62-67, 126
    blocking technique, 64
    cyanide used in, 65-66
    ingredients of, 63
    procedure, 64-66
    purpose of, 63
cast, 16, 25. See also bend
cast-off, 22, 25
cast-on, 22, 25

INDEX

chamber brush, 177
Charles Daly Model 500, 151
cheekpiece stocks, 5
Churchill guns, 3, 48, 169
cleaning rod, 176
cocking rods, 53
Cogswell & Harrision guns, 169
coin finish, 165
comb drop, 23-24

D
Daly, Charles, 151
Damascus barrels, 35, 36, 37
  (illustr.), 38, 118-120, 128,
  136, 150
    volatility of, 118
    restoration of, 120
Damascus steel, 99
Darne guns, 135
deep relief engraving, 94, 110-112
Definitive Proof, 43
Devimers guns, 134
diamond grip, 83
Dickson guns, 150-151,169
    triple-barreled, 150
    "Round Action," 150
Dickson, John, 150
diecasting, 10
double guns, 1-11, 29
    early design of, 1, 24-25
    for driven-bird shooting, 8
    mounting of, 8
    caring for, 69
    side-by-side smoothbore, 29
double triggers, 56
driven-bird shooting, 8, 13

E
Eibar, Spain, 133
ejector guns, problems with, 123, 124
engraver's pitch, 100
engraving, 93-112
    machine engravers, 95
    techniques, 98, 102-112

    single-stroke fine scroll, 102
    drop spec fine scroll, 102
    reverse bevel, 109
    deep-relief, 110-112
  styles, 94
  tools, 97-98
extractor channel, 41

F
Fabbri guns, 148, 149
Famars guns, 148, 149
Ferlach guns, Austria, 133
FERLIB guns, 148, 149
fiber wads, 126
Forbes guns, 151
forcing cones, 126
fore-end furniture, 53
fore-end iron, 57
    function of, 57
    production, 57
fore-end loop, 39, 41
Fox guns, 4, 9, 26, 128-129, 169
    beavertail forearms in, 128
    ejectors in, 128
    limitations of, 128
    maintenance of, 129
    non-rebounding hammers in, 12
    options offered for, 128
    rotary-bolting design of, 128
    single-selective triggers in, 128
Fox, Ansley H., 128
Francotte guns, 137-138
French grey finish, 165
French gunmaking, 133, 134-136
French walnut, 71, 72, 134
    Perigord region, 135-136
funeral gun, 47-48

G
game gun handling, 3, 6-7 (illustr.)
game gun design, 4, 5
    English influences of, 5
    French, 5
    German and Austrian, 5

Armas Garbi 133, 141-142, 144
    100 CF, 144 (illustr.)
    100, 144 (illustr.)
    101CC, 144 (illustr.)
    103A Special, 142 (illustr.)
German guns, 5, 133, 160
    characteristics of, 145, 146
glossary of terms, 185-191
Granger, Georges, 134
Granger guns, 133, 134-135
Grant guns, 169
Greener crossbolt, 138, 146, 160
gun care accessories, 170-180
gun case, 170-173
    styles, 172
gun cleaning, 176-178, 180, 181-182
gun cloths, 180
gunfit, 14-27, 30
    measuring for, 14, 22
gun mounting techniques, 3, 5, 18, 23, 26-27, 29
    English method, 18
    thrust-forward method, 23
    pointing, 29
    stance, 21
gun repair, 175-176
gun selection, 166
gun storage, 173
    prolonged, 182
gun weight, 161-162
gunmaking, contemporary, 13, 33-69, 71-81, 84-90, 94-104, 108-110, 113, 162, 164
    CAD/CAM used in, 161
    decline of, 15, 134
    international centers of, 133
        American, 8, 9, 44
        Austrian, 146-14
        Belgian, 136-138
        English, 9, 154-155, 157-160
        French, 134-136
        German, 145-146
        Italian, 147-150
        Japanese, 151-154
        Scottish, 150-151
        Spanish, 139-145
    mass production, 4
    modern methods, 10
    overview of, 33-34
gunmaking, history of, 9, 33, 117-130, 134, 136, 169
    American, 4-5, 9-10, 117, 118, 120, 126, 128, 130
    English, 1-2, 3-4, 9, 38, 56, 94, 156
    French, 5, 134
    Belgian, 136

H
hand guards, 178
hand-detachable locks, 175
hanger, 39-41
head-space problems, 68
heel-toe twist, 26
Henry guns, 151
hinged triggers, 54
Holland & Holland guns, 3, 9, 103, 110, 155, 165, 169
Hollis guns, 169
Hoppes No. 9, 181

I
inlay, 104-110
    materials, 110
    techniques, 105 (illustr.), 106-107 (illustr.), 108
    overlay, 109-110
international style shooting, 144
Italian guns, 133, 147-151
    characterisitcs of, 148, 149
    over-under, 160
Ithaca guns, 130, 169
    Japanese-made, 151

Index

J
J. P. Sauer & Sons guns, 146
J. Woodward & Sons, 158, 159, 160
Woodward guns
    12-gauge, 168 (illustr.)
James Purdey & Sons, 62. *See also*
Purdey guns
Japanese gunmaking, 151-154
    history of, 151

K
Kentucky muzzleloader, 4
Kersten-type crossbolt, 160
Krupp barrels, 128

L
L. C. Smith guns, 4, 69, 114
  (illustr.), 129-130, 160, 169
Lancaster guns, 169
Lang guns, 169
laser inletting, 10
Lebeau-Courally guns, 138
Lefaucheaux guns, 134
Lefever guns, 4, 5, 9, 26, 130, 169
Lefever, Dan, 5
leg vise, 100
length of pull, 14
Liège, Belgium, 133
lockmaking, 58-62
London Gunmaker's Company, 42

M
Manton, Joseph, 1, 10
Merkel guns, 145-146
Miroku, B. C., 151
Mortimer & Sons guns, 151
muzzleloader, 1, 4
    side-by-side, 1
    early American, 4,

O
oil bottles, 174
    oval grip, 83
over-under, 157-167
    design concerns, 158
    history of, 157-158

innovations, 159-160
Italian makers of, 160
limitations, 167
manufacturing procedures,
    162-164

P
Parker gun, 4, 5, 9, 26, 118-127, 169
    "Old Reliable", 5, 118
    A-1 Special, 4, 121 (illustr.)
    AHE Grade 16-gauge,
      125 (Illustr.)
    DHE Grade 12-gauge, two-
      barreled, 123
    DHE Grade 20-gauge, 118
      (illustr.), 153-154
    Invincible, 103
    Trojan Grades, 127
    reproductions, 153-154
Parker, Charles S., 5, 118, 121. *See also* Parker gun
Perrazi guns, 148, 150
phosphor bronze brushes, 177-178
Piotti guns, 133, 148, 149
    Model King No. 1, 149
    Model King Extra, 143 (illustr.)
    Model Lunik, 149
pitch, 16, 25-26
plastic cup wads, 126
Purdey guns, 3, 9, 155
    16-gauge, 154 (illustr.)
    20-gauge over-under,
      156 (illustr.)
    over-under, 159-160, 165
pushrod fastener device, 57

R
receiver hardware, 53
recoil pads, 179
recoil, 24, 25, 41, 54, 56
Remington guns, 130
repeating shotguns, 5
ribs, 40-41

201

Richards, Westley, 56, 120, 155
riders, 164
rifle-shotgun combination, 5
Rizzini guns, 148, 149
Roosevelt, Theodore, 128
rose-and-scroll engraving, 94
Ruger Red Label, 162-164

S

safety catch, 53
Scottish guns, 150-151
semi-pistol-grip stocks, 5
Sharp single-shot, 4
shotgun design, 5
    American, 8
    German and Austrian, 5
    influences of, 4
shotgunning, history of, 5
"shooting flying," 5
side-by-side, 5, 27, 28-29
    advantages of, 167
    in upland hunting, 8
pistol-grip, 5
    Remington, 5
    best-quality, 8
    aspects of, 8
sidelock gun, 1, 5, 58, 129
    self-opening, 54-56
    assisted opening, 54-56
    double rife, 55 (illustr.)
    side-by-side, 27
    components, 58
    production, 58-59
    intercepting sears, 59-60
    Lefever, 5
single-selective triggers. 56, 165
single sighting plane, 29
single triggers, 56, 165
    on Winchester Model 21, 56
16-gauge game gun, 27, 28, 30
    side-by-side, 27
SKB guns
    Model 100, 152
    Model 200, 152
    Model 280, 152
    side-by-side, 152
sleeved barrels, 38
sling mounts, 5
Smith, L. C., 9. *See also*
  L. C. Smith guns
snap caps, 173-174
Sodia, Franz, 146
solvent storage, 174
Southgate ejector system, 57
Spain, 139
Spanish guns, 133, 139-145
Special Edition Winchester
  Model 23, 8
splinter-forearmed shotgun, 5
square load, 27
"suck fit," 164
St. Etienne, France, 133
stack barrels, 158. *See also*
  over-under
stock design, English, 13
stock, 8, 74-76, 82-90
    cast, 74-75
    cast-on, 75
    cast-off, 75
    checkering, 85-90
        tools for, 87
    drop dimensions, 75-76
    finishing, 84-85
    fit, 26-27, 30, 82-84
    grip design, 83
stockmaking, 71-90,
    procedures, 73-76, 80-81
        inletting, 76, 80-81
    tools, 76
    wood used in, 71-73, 78
straight-grip stock, 3, 5
    benefits of, 3, 5
    in British guns, 5
    in early American guns, 5
striker bottles, 175

Index

Suhl, Germany, 133, 145-146
super-imposed, 158. *See also*
 over-under
"Sweet Elsie", 130. *See also*
 L. C. Smith
T
"thickness of smoke," 38 (illustr.),
 41, 42, 52
tompons, 178
"top hat" shooting, 3-4
top lever, 53
trigger guard, 53
trigger-guard bow and strap, 54
trigger-pull, 56
triggers, 53, 54
try-gun, 14, 16-22
turnscrews, 175-176
U
universal tilt vise, 100
V
vertical tubes, 158. *See also*
 over-under
Vouzland guns, 135-136
 Anson-and-Deeley-style action
  in, 135
 third grip in, 135
 receivers in, 135
 chopper-lump barrels in, 135
W
W. & C. Scott, 155
water table, 42. *See also* action
flats
Webley & Scott, 135
Whitworth, Sir Joseph, 36
Wilkes, John, 103
Winchester guns,
 Japanese-made, 151, 152-154
 lever-action, 4
 Model 12, 5
 Model 21 Grand American, 48,
  56, 130, 151, 165
 Model 23, 153
wingshooting, history of, 134
wood creep, 123
wood pidgeons, 4
Woodward guns, 158, 159, 160
Worshipful Master Gunbuilder's
 Guild, 53